THINGS TO DO IN THE UPPER PENINSULA BEFORE YOU DIE

100
THINGS TO DO IN
THE UPPER PENINSULA
BEFORE YOU
DIE

•••••••••••••••••••••••••••••

KATH USITALO

Reedy Press
PO Box 5131
St. Louis, MO 63139, USA
www.reedypress.com

Library of Congress Control Number: 9781681060569

ISBN: 2016940402

Design by Jill Halpin

All Images: Kath Usitalo

Printed in the United States of America
17 18 19 20 21   5 4 3

DEDICATION

To TJ, Graham, and Paige and the miles we've traveled together, and the miles we've yet to go.

CONTENTS

• •

Music and Entertainment

Sports and Recreation

• •

Culture and History

Fashion and Shopping

PREFACE

In photos from space, it looks as though the Upper Peninsula belongs to that landmass west of Lake Michigan called Wisconsin. But despite the long, shared border and preponderance of Packers fans in the UP, the state line was decided during the Toledo War of 1835-36. You can look up the sordid details, but the upshot is that the Michigan Territory lost a boundary dispute over a slip of land—the "Toledo Strip"—and received the consolation prize of the seemingly worthless UP. Thank you, Ohio.

It wasn't long before the UP's wealth of natural resources was revealed. And now its recreational, historical, and cultural assets are being discovered by a growing number of visitors who venture to this vast, off-the-beaten-path swath of land. Even the dictionary recognizes Yoopers, the hardy residents with the self-reliant, independent spirit required to thrive in a sparsely populated wilderness surrounded on three sides by massive inland seas. A place short on summer but long on scenic beauty and quirky personality.

It's difficult for first-time visitors to grasp the distances between the towns, parks, attractions—basically everything—in the UP. A bit of advice: plan your trip and cut in half the amount you think you'll be able to see. This book covers 100 Things, but it only scratches the surface. You need to allow time for making discoveries along the way, and you won't want to rush. Yoopers do not rush.

• •

Things to keep in mind as you travel the UP:

- Many businesses and attractions are seasonal—usually meaning sometime in May to sometime in October.
- Bring some cash for those places that do not accept credit cards.
- The UP has one area code (906) but two time zones; it's mostly Eastern but along the Wisconsin border there's a zig-zag area on Central time.
- GPS is sometimes confusing. Pick up paper maps for back-up navigation.
- Before exploring on backroads, be aware that some are better suited to SUVs and four-wheel drive than sedans.
- For visitor information, consult the Upper Peninsula Travel & Recreation Association at uptravel.com, and the state's Pure Michigan office at michigan.org.
- Visit the state's staffed welcome centers for a wealth of free information and travel tips at Iron Mountain, Ironwood, Marquette, Menominee, St. Ignace, and Sault Ste. Marie: michigan.gov/mdot.

Welcome to da UP, eh!

• •

ACKNOWLEDGMENTS

Many thanks to the Yoopers, Wannabe Yoopers, and Ex-Pat Yoopers for your *100 Things* suggestions, and for your passion for this special place. I will always appreciate my family—siblings, parents, cousins, aunts, uncles, and grandparents (many sadly gone) who are so much a part of the experiences and memories I have of vacations spent in the UP. That's when my dream of living above the Bridge began. It took me a while (as everything does with me), but I'm so happy to finally be living here, working to earn my Yooper stripes.

FOOD AND DRINK

1

SEE MONKS JAM
IN THE WILDERNESS

Father Basil and Father Nicholas had a fledgling monastery to support and no skills to bring income to their isolated spot on the Lake Superior shore. But with a bounty of wild blueberries, raspberries, strawberries, and thimbleberries outside their door, the monks of the Society of St. John learned to turn foraged fruits into jams, jellies, butters, and preserves. Decades later, in the cozy Jampot bakery and shop next to pretty little Jacob Creek Falls, jars of their handcrafted Poorrock Abbey spreads fly off the shelves, and lines form for fresh-from-the-oven bakery treats like molasses cookies, pumpkin muffins, and luscious brownies. The good-humored, brown-cloaked monks walk across the road from the onion-domed monastery to make and sell their wares at the Jampot from May through mid-October (closed Sundays), and online throughout the year.

6500 M-26, Eagle Harbor 49950
store.societystjohn.com/Jampot

TIP

Yoopers like to make and sell small batches of jams at farm markets and roadside stops, like the Jam Lady's well-signed shop near Eagle River.

5055 M-26, Mohawk 49950, 906-337-4164
thimbleberryjamlady.com

2

GET YOUR JOLT
AT JAVA JOE'S

The roadside joint painted in a rainbow of colors is straight out of Margaritaville, but coffee is the strongest pour at this St. Ignace diner with a hippy-dippy 'tude. When Java Joe's Café opened in 1999, it brought a funky vibe to Michigan's second oldest city. Good luck choosing from the fluffy pancakes, mouthwatering omelets, and inventive crepes (think paper-thin buckwheat pancake stuffed with turkey, avocado, bacon, pico de gallo, and cheese). Breakfast is popular all day, but the sandwiches and pizza win raves as well. The cozy, brightly painted interior is lined with shelves of teapots and cookie jars for sale along with snapshots of the brave souls who've tackled humongous servings of the signature strawberry shortcake or brownie combinations topped with ice cream AND whipped cream.

959 N. State St., St. Ignace 49781, 906-643-5282
facebook.com/Java-Joes-Cafe-150762761856/

3

EAT LIKE A MINER,
DIG INTO A PASTY

If the UP had an official food, it would be the pasty. Not to be confused with racy lingerie, these PASS-tees are the hearty meat and root vegetable pies brought by Cornish miners in the mid-1800s. The solid, all-in-one meal has outlived the copper and iron mining booms and now comes in vegetarian, chicken, breakfast, and even dessert varieties—although pasty purists insist on the traditional combination of beef, potatoes, onions, rutabaga and/or carrots wrapped in a flaky but substantial crust. Yoopers are particular about pasties, inspiring fierce loyalties and debates about whether to top them with ketchup, gravy, or just a pat of butter. One favorite pasty shop is Muldoons in Munising. Step inside the sunny yellow house, inhale the aroma of hot-from-the-oven pasties, and try not to drool.

Muldoons
1246 M-28 W., Munising 49862, 906-387-5880
muldoonspasties.com
Seasonal

NOTE

Some pasty shops are open only during the warm weather months, but there's no shortage of year-round options across the UP.

Connie's Kitchen

56901 S. 6th St., Calumet 49913, 906-337-0113
facebook.com/Connies-Kitchen-357237371052/

Crossroads Restaurant & Lounge

900 County Rd. 480, Marquette 49855, 906-249-8912
facebook.com/Crossroads-Restaurant-Lounge-130167517064131/

Hiawatha Pasties

W11644 US-2, Naubinway 49762, 906-477-1148
facebook.com/HiawathaPasties

The Hut Inn

58542 Wolverine St. (US-41), Calumet 49913, 906-337-1133
hutinn.com

Lehto's Pasties Since 1947

W1983 US-2, St. Ignace 49781, 906-643-8542
lehtospasties.com

BE A FUDGIE
ON MACKINAC ISLAND

Every summer day, Northern Michigan visitors—known as fudgies—consume and carry away thousands of pounds of fudge from Mackinac Island sweet shops. The fudge phenomenon began in 1887 when home fudge maker Sara Murdick's husband and son opened a candy kitchen to tempt the island's blossoming tourist trade. Today, multiple fudge shops have turned fudge-making into candy shop performance art, cooking their special combinations of sugar, cream, butter, chocolate, and flavorings in copper kettles, then cooling and paddling the mix into loaves on marble-topped tables and slicing the candy into half-pound slabs. Fans blow the intoxicating aroma into the streets, and free samples are plentiful. Be a fudgie, and try them all before you buy. And you will buy.

Grand Hotel
grandhotel.com

Joann's Fudge
joannsfudge.com

May's Candy Shops
maysfudge.com

Murdick's Fudge
originalmurdicksfudge.com

Murray Hotel Fudge Company
mymurrayhotel.com

Ryba's Fudge
ryba.com

Sanders Candy
sanderscandy.com

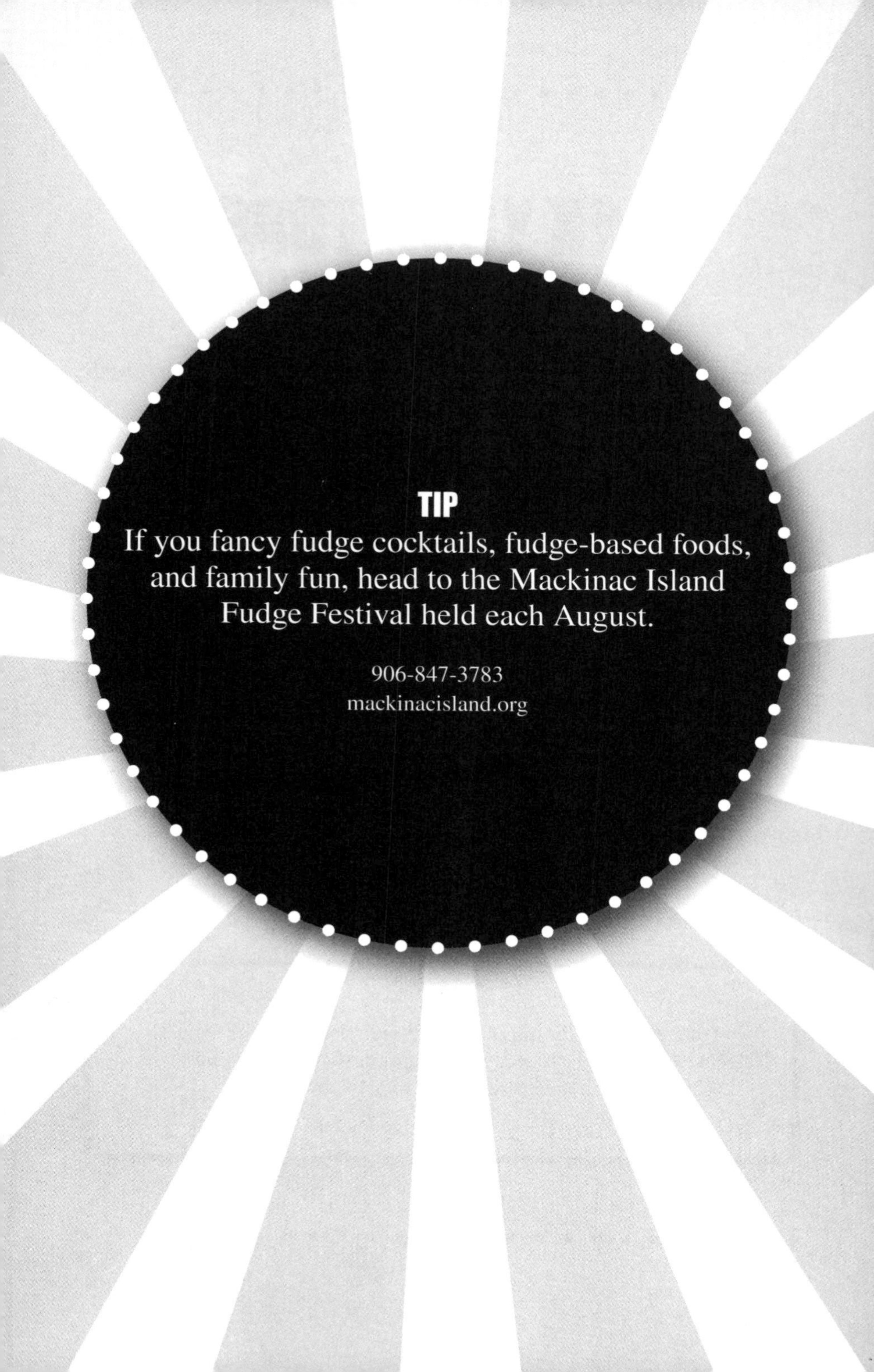
TIP
If you fancy fudge cocktails, fudge-based foods, and family fun, head to the Mackinac Island Fudge Festival held each August.
906-847-3783
mackinacisland.org

5

DUNK YOUR TOAST
AT TRENARY HOME BAKERY

Generations of Yoopers have grown up on this version of Finnish korppu, the thick, crunchy slices of twice-baked bread coated with cinnamon sugar that Trenary Home Bakery has been turning out since 1928. The toast is dunked quickly in a cup of coffee or broken into chunks in a bowl of milk to soften it and bring out the flavor. In addition to the traditional cinnamon, Trenary Toast comes in plain, vanilla, cinnamon-raisin, and cardamom varieties. You'll find it, packed in plain brown paper bags, on grocery shelves across the UP. Or head to the tiny mid-peninsula town of Trenary to stock up at the source. Have a freshly baked cinnamon roll and coffee and maybe a toast-dunking lesson in the café that fronts the bakery.

E-2918 M-67, Trenary 49891, 906-446-3330
trenaryhomebakery.com

TIP

Time your visit for the end of February and catch the annual Trenary Outhouse Classic, when teams push decorated outhouses down main street. Beer may be involved.

trenaryouthouseclassic.com

6

SUP ON THE SUPERIOR SHORE
AT FITZGERALD'S

The northern tip of the UP is probably the last place you'd expect to find Southern-style barbecue—very good barbecue smoked daily with local hardwood. But that's not the only surprise in store at Fitzgerald's, steps from Lake Superior in Eagle River. Add carefully chosen whiskeys from around the world and craft beer on tap and in bottles. The Fitz beverage list is longer than the innovative menu of fresh fish, burgers, and vegetarian entrees, along with the specialty ribs, brisket, and pulled pork. Large windows line the cozy dining room so that everyone has a breathtaking view of the other-worldly sunsets, miles of whitecaps, or even the fierce storms that grace this special spot on the Keweenaw Peninsula.

5033 Front St., Eagle River 49950, 906-337-0666
fitzgeralds-mi.com
Seasonal

TIP

Book a waterfront room upstairs at the Eagle River Inn. With the Lake Superior sights and sounds outside your window, you'll never turn on your flat screen TV.

7

DRIVE IN
FOR CLYDE'S BIG C

They've been flipping burgers at Clyde's Drive-Ins since 1949, when the first joint opened in Sault Ste. Marie. The #2 Clyde's is in Manistique; the third location in St. Ignace is independent of the mini-chain, but all serve the same juicy burgers, fries, and shakes. Freshly ground and hand-pressed patties are grilled as quarter-pounders and stacked three on a bun to create Clyde's colossal "Big C" burger. Top it with pickle chips, chopped onions, and Velveeta cheese if you want the enhanced burger experience. The roller-skating carhops are a thing of the past, but curb service is an option at these UP institutions.

201 Chippewa Ave., Manistique 49854, 906-341-6021
https://www.facebook.com/Clydes-Drive-In-Manistique-121120881237712/

906 US-2 W, St. Ignace 49781, 906-643-8303
https://www.facebook.com/Clydes-178349385561991/

1425 Riverside Dr., Sault Ste. Marie 49783, 906-632-2581
https://www.facebook.com/pages/Clydes-Drive-In/111576548878179?fref=ts

TIP
The Soo and St. Ignace locations are seasonal, but you can get your Big C fix year-round at Clyde's in Manistique.

8

CHOW DOWN
ON CUDIGHI

It's a spicy pork sausage brought to the UP by immigrants from northern Italy, and it's pretty much remained a Yooper food found largely in the Iron Mountain and Ishpeming areas. Cudighi (pronounced coo-dig-ee or cud-i-gee) is flavored with varying combinations of cinnamon, nutmeg, cloves, and allspice—each kitchen has its special recipe. It's a popular topping on the thin crust, brick oven pies at Congress Pizza, an Ishpeming institution since 1934. At nearby Ralph's Italian Deli, a restaurant and Italian foods market, you can buy cudighi in mild, medium, or hot varieties by the pound, or grilled in a sandwich. The tasty patty comes on a homemade roll under the unlikely combination of mozzarella cheese, mustard, ketchup, and onion. Go all out and add the house-made pizza sauce.

Congress Pizza
106 N. Main St., Ispheming 49849, 906-486-4233
facebook.com/congresspizzas

Ralph's Italian Deli
601 Palms Ave. at US-41, Ishpeming 49849, 906-485-4557
ralphsitaliandeli.com

9

CATCH YOUR FILL
OF WHITEFISH

Yoopers were eating local long before it became a foodie trend. Whitefish straight from the cold, deep waters of Lakes Michigan and Superior has been a UP staple for centuries. Favored for its mild flavor and flaky texture, the versatile catch shows up at fish fries and on menus everywhere as dips, chowder, sandwiches, and entrees broiled, baked, grilled, and pan fried. Generations-old family fish markets sell their fresh catch filleted and in glistening hunks smoked UP-style: skin on, over a hot hardwood fire. Stop at Gustafson's in tiny Brevort for a chunk of whitefish fresh from the roadside smoker, grab a sleeve of saltine crackers, and head to a nearby Lake Michigan beach for a hyperlocal snack.

TIP

Whitefish may not be available in the winter if ice prevents the boats from going out.

Gustafson's Smoked Fish
Variety of fresh fish smoked on-site; good jerky, too

W4467 US-2, Brevort 49760, 906-292-5424
gustafsonssmokedfishinc.com

Peterson's Fish Market and Four Suns Fish & Chips Outdoor Café
Year-round market with fresh and smoked fish, casual meals at seasonal café

49813N US-41, Hancock 49930, 906-482-2343
facebook.com/Petersonfishmarket/

Timmy Lee's Pub
Lightly battered and seasoned whitefish nibblets, whitefish Reuben on rye

W748 US-2, St. Ignace 49781, 906-643-8344
facebook.com/Timmy-Lees-Pub-206451249386432/?fref=ts

Thill's Fish House
Fresh and smoked Lake Superior fish sold retail from a waterside Quonset hut

250 E. Main St., Marquette 49855, 906-226-9851
facebook.com/Thills-Fish-House-133945293391376/

GET FED
BY A FUTURE TOP CHEF

The setting is rustic, the food refined, and the reviews are rave at Les Cheneaux Culinary School Restaurant in Hessel, a resort village in the Eastern UP. Operation of the restaurant serves as a hands-on internship for the small class of chefs completing their one-year program at the school, which was established in 2014. The fine dining focus is on the wealth of local food suppliers and natural resources, from trout to pork, to dairy and produce. The casual dining room has the feel of the old boat houses that dot the channels of the island archipelago outside the door. Nab the Chef's Table or enjoy the deck with views of the water. The restaurant is open only during the summer, with occasional theme dinners through the fall and winter months.

186 S. Pickford Ave., Hessel 49745, 906-484-4800
lcculinary.org

TASTE TRADITION
AT RIVERSIDE PIZZERIA

Loyal customers claim that pizza that's been cut into squares instead of wedges has fewer calories, and that's why it's done that way at Riverside Bar & Pizzeria, which has been serving its thin crust pies since 1946. Baked in stone deck ovens and topped with a family secret sauce, the menu offers ten simple combinations of sausage, pepperoni, onions, mushrooms, and cheese, with wildcard pepperoncini on #8. The new generation has added—almost as an aside—green pepper and pineapple toppings, as well as a gluten-free crust option. Also new since 1946: free Wi-Fi—probably to entertain the ever-present crowds waiting for a booth or stool at the bar.

98 E. Genesee St., Iron River 49935, 906-265-9944
riverside-pizzeria.com

TIP

Try the pizza "extra cheese out."

DOWN SOME HISTORY
AT UP BREWPUBS

In 1883, Martin Vierling opened his saloon at the corner of Front and Main Streets in downtown Marquette. A century later, the doors swung open again on a restaurant and "sampling room" refurbished with a period oak bar, wooden booths, exposed brick walls, and stained glass accent pieces and oil paintings that belonged to Vierling himself. The reinvented Vierling Restaurant & Marquette Harbor Brewery is known for the whitefish that shows up as appetizers, chowder, and entrées, but there's enough variety on the extensive menu to satisfy everyone. On the lower level of the building, the Vierling brewmaster turns out small batches of beer that are available only at the historic establishment.

The Vierling Restaurant & Marquette Harbor Brewery
119 S. Front St., Marquette 49855, 906-228-3533
thevierling.com

TIP

Ask for a table overlooking the Lake Superior harbor.

Here's a sampling of UP brewpubs that serve a side of history with their food and specialty beers:

Hereford & Hops Steakhouse and Brewpub
Choose-and-grill your own steaks; burgers and pizza

624 Ludington St., Escanaba 49829, 906-789-1945
herefordandhops.com

Lake Superior Brewing Company at the Dunes Saloon
BBQ ribs, pizza, and whitefish in summer from the big lake down the street

N-14283 Lake Ave., Grand Marais 49839, 906-494-2337
facebook.com/Lake-Superior-Brewing-Company-72923808780

Michigan House Café & Red Jacket Brewing Co.
Grilled Lake Superior trout, Gipp Burger named for local hero, "The Gipper"

300 6th St., Calumet 49913, 906-337-1910
michiganhousecafe.com

Tahquamenon Falls Brewery & Pub
Wild rice soup, brew pub sausage sandwich, steaks, whitefish

Tahquamenon Falls State Park, 41382 W. M-123, Paradise 49768, 906-492-3300
tahquamenonfallsbrewery.com

13

SANDWICH IN A STOP FOR EATS
IN MANISTIQUE

Buzz through Manistique, a Lake Michigan lumber and paper mill town on US-2, and you'll miss out on two tasty sandwich spots just off the highway. Detour to the Upper Crust Deli's airy, waterside dining room for a relaxing lunch—good luck choosing from the menu's nearly 30 made-to-order sandwiches on a choice of homemade breads. Save room for a cookie fresh from the oven. At Cedar Street Café in the business district, local art hangs on the stripped-down brick walls, good java brews at the coffee bar, and the menu tempts with decadent Heavenly French Toast (it involves caramel, pecans, and whipped cream) and lunch choices like Cuban panini and Greek chicken wrap.

Cedar Street Café and Coffeehouse
220 S. Cedar St., Manistique 49854, 906-341-2469
cedarstreetcafe.com

Upper Crust Deli
375 Traders' Point Dr., Manistique 49854, 906-341-2253
facebook.com/uppercrustdeli99

14

CAROUSE WITH THE GNOMES
AT THE AMBASSADOR

The Keweenaw Peninsula's Bosch Brewing Company is long gone, but murals commissioned by Joseph Bosch live on at the Ambassador, a historic barroom in downtown Houghton. In 1902 an artist named Rohrbeck painted the scenes of drinking, singing, and beer-making bearded gnomes for the Giltedge, another local bar. Over the decades the canvases were stashed away, and in the 1940s or '50s installed in the Ambassador's cocoon-like curved ceiling. "The Ambo" is a college town hangout for Michigan Tech students, visiting alumni, and locals who devour meatball sandwiches and thin-crust pizza. Try the Mexican-inspired tostada pizza topped with spiced ground beef, cheese, lettuce, tomatoes, and hot sauce. Neon colored, 25-ounce fishbowl drinks are the signature sip.

126 Sheldon Ave., Houghton 49931, 906-482-5054
theambassadorhoughton.com

15

TIP A FEW UP BREWS

Beer fans are finding it a fun challenge to stay on top of the growing craft beer scene in the UP. These are some of the taprooms across the Yoop where you'll find house-made brews:

Blackrocks Brewery
424 N. 3rd St., Marquette 49855, 906-273-1333
blackrocksbrewery.com

Brickside Brewery
64 Gratiot St., Copper Harbor 49918, 906-289-4772
facebook.com/bricksidebrew/

Cognition Brewing Company
113 E. Canda St., Ishpeming 49849, 906-204-2724
facebook.com/CognitionBrewingCompany

Keweenaw Brewing Company
408 Shelden Ave., Houghton 49931, 906-482-5596
kbc.beer

Ore Dock Brewing Company
114 Spring St., Marquette 49855, 906-228-8888
ore-dock.com

Soo Brewing Company
223 W. Portage Ave., Sault Ste. Marie 49783, 906-632-4400
soobrew.com

Upper Hand Brewery
3525 Airport Rd., Escanaba 49829, 906-233-5005
upperhandbrewery.com

ORE DOCK
BREWING COMPANY
MARQUETTE, MICHIGAN

EAT UP
IN THE UP FOODIE CAPITAL

Taste buds are exploding in Marquette. Local palates no longer have to be satisfied with college town pizza and the hearty, meat-and-potato fare associated with cold climes, a short growing season, and costly logistics of moving food to the Lake Superior shore. When it opened in 1993, Sweet Water Café was a culinary pioneer with its locally sourced, organic, vegetarian, and multicultural menu. Now, even the food trucks have pulled into town, and Marquette is on a roll as the cuisine capital of the UP.

BabyCakes Muffin Company
Great coffee and good-for-you breakfast, lunch, and baked goods

223 W. Washington St., Marquette 49855, 906-226-7744
facebook.com/babycakesmqt

Dia de los Tacos
Roving food truck serves meat, vegetarian, and gluten-free tacos

906-361-3740
facebook.com/DiaDeLosTacos

Elizabeth's Chop House
Worth-the-splurge prime rib, lamb chops, surf and turf

113 S. Front St., Marquette 49855, 906-228-0900
elizabethschophouse.com

Huron Mountain Bakery
Great Lakes themed sandwiches, two dozen breads by the loaf, plus sweets

1301 S. Front St., Marquette 49855, 906-225-1301
huronmountainbakery.com

Jilbert Dairy Farm Store
Because everyone needs to try the local ice cream at the big cow

200 Meeske Ave., Marquette 49855, 906-225-1363
jilbertdairy.com

Lagniappe Cajun Creole Eatery and Voodoo Bar
Authentic, from-scratch taste of Louisiana

145 Washington St., Marquette 49855, 906-226-8200
marquettecajun.com

Zephyr Bar
Wine by the glass or bottle, tasty small plates

215 S. Front St., Marquette 49855, 906-225-5470
facebook.com/UPwinebar

GET SWEET ON A ROLL
FIT FOR PAUL BUNYAN

Weighing in at about a pound, the Hilltop Restaurant's cinnamon rolls have made the village of L'Anse a destination and a detour-inducing stop for more than 60 years. On a typical weekend the kitchen will go through 3,000 pounds of flour, 150 pounds of sugar, 60 pounds of apples, 300 pounds of powdered sugar, and lots and lots of cinnamon to meet the demand for the giant-sized sweet rolls, made from a family recipe. You could get one to-go, but this towering, plate-sized treat is best eaten warm from the oven while seated at a table, with utensils to scoop up the drippy icing, and a glass of milk to wash it all down.

18047 US-41, L'Anse 49946, 906-524-7858
sweetroll.com

FEAST ON ALMOST FAMOUS RIBS
AT THE UP NORTH LODGE

No need to wait until they hit the big time. The "almost" world famous BBQ ribs are a crowd favorite at The Up North Lodge near Gwinn, about 20 miles south of Marquette. Racks of fall-off-the-bone ribs are the specialty, but the extensive menu tries to satisfy every appetite. The handsome log structure oozes UP ambience with its rustic decor, fireplace, pool table, friendly vibe at the bar, and wall of windows overlooking the wooded setting. While in the area, take a spin through Gwinn to see traces of the "Model Town" designed and built more than a century ago by Cleveland-Cliffs Iron Company for its mining families.

215 S. County Rd. 557, Gwinn 49841, 906-346-9815
theupnorthlodge.com

STUFF YOURSELF
AT THE ANTLERS

The deer and the antelope no longer play at The Antlers: the critters are among a few hundred mounted racks and taxidermied specimens that stare down at diners from the walls, ceiling, and overhead beams of this Sault Ste. Marie institution. Menu favorites include Michigan Gumbo, a mash-up of local whitefish with the traditional sausage, chicken, and okra; the full-pound Paul Bunyan Burger; and poutine, a pile of hand-cut fries topped with cheese curds and gravy (slab of venison meatloaf optional). The former Bucket of Blood Saloon posed as a Prohibition-era ice cream parlor until the feds got wise. The next owners populated the place with stuffed animals of the wild kind, from big cats, beaver, birds, and moose, to a polar bear and a two-headed calf.

804 E. Portage Ave., Sault Ste. Marie 49783, 906-253-1728
sooantlers.com

ROAST A WIENIE,
DRINK BEER,
REPEAT

Sometimes, the simplest meals can be the most satisfying. Yoopers like to jab wieners and big fat sausages onto sturdy sticks and roast them over an open fire, preferably at the lakeshore. Eat 'em with mustard and wash 'em down with beer. Vollwerth's natural casing wieners, ring bologna, and variety of sausages are bonfire favorites, made in the UP and found at markets across the peninsula. Richard Vollwerth, newly arrived from Germany, started his sausage company in 1915 in Hancock, where generations three, four, and five continue to use the brick-lined, Old World smokehouse and century-old recipes of the "King of Meats."

For store locations: vollwerth.com

KITCH-ITI-KIPI
.....THE BIG SPRING
You Are Here

MUSIC AND ENTERTAINMENT

21

STROLL THROUGH A JUNKYARD ART PARK
AT LAKENENLAND

Tom Lakenen has a day job in construction and is a member of the Boilermaker's Union, but years ago, when he gave up beer, he needed something to occupy his free time. So he put his welding skills to use making metal sculptures from scrap iron: big sculptures, like monsters and dinosaurs, colorful critters, and (he says) "all the things I saw while drinking." The self-taught artist bought acreage where he could share his works—more than 80 to date—in a free sculpture park (donations are appreciated) located 15 miles east of Marquette. Lakenenland is open all day, every day, all year round, for the enjoyment of hikers, snowmobilers, families, and anyone who appreciates that one man's trash can be another man's junkyard art.

2800 M-28 E., Marquette 49855, 906-249-1132
lakenenland.com

22

GO OLD HOLLYWOOD
AND TRACK THE ANATOMY OF A MURDER

A scandalous, true tale of lust, revenge, and murder in a small UP town inspired local defense attorney John D. Voelker, under the pen name Robert Traver, to write the novel *Anatomy of a Murder*. His best-seller was made into the 1959 movie of the same name, filmed on location in and around Marquette with stars James Stewart, Lee Remick, Ben Gazzara, Eve Arden, and Arthur O'Connell. Movie buffs will want to pick up a self-guided tour brochure from the tourism office and trace film locations in Marquette, Ishpeming, and Big Bay, the scene of the crime. The Marquette County courtroom used in the film is rich with mahogany woodwork, and the stained-glass dome is stunning as well.

Marquette County Convention & Visitors Bureau
117 W. Washington St., Marquette 49855, 800-544-4321 or 906-228-7749
travelmarquettemichigan.com

TIP

Have a meal or stay the night at Thunder Bay Inn in Big Bay, a hotel and film location once owned by Henry Ford, who used it when visiting the Ford plant in town.

400 Bensinger, Big Bay 49808, 906-345-9220
thunderbayinn.net

GUSH
OVER WATERFALLS

The number of UP waterfalls is a matter of debate because so many are unnamed, inaccessible, or qualify more as rapids. But it's safe to say there are at least 200 falls, from minor to magnificent. The largest, Tahquamenon Falls in the Eastern UP, is 200 feet wide with a 50-foot drop; the gentler Lower Falls are four miles downstream. As you head west across the UP, you'll find some falls a short stroll from the road, others a backcountry hike away. Standouts that are relatively easy to access include Bond Falls on the Ontonagon River, a series of five falls along the 12-mile Black River National Forest Scenic Byway, and Sturgeon Falls and Sturgeon River Gorge Wilderness, Michigan's "Grand Canyon," with walls up to 300 feet high.

Search UP waterfalls at uptravel.com

TIP

Check with local tourism offices for maps and directions to falls in the area you're visiting.

Black River National Forest Scenic Byway
Five waterfalls in Ironwood area

906-932-4850
westernup.com/waterfalls/briver.html

Bond Falls Scenic Site

Bond Falls Rd., Paulding, 906-353-6558
michigan.gov/dnr

Sturgeon Falls, Sturgeon River Gorge Wilderness

Ottawa National Forest, Sidnaw area
906-932-1330
fs.usda.gov

Tahquamenon Falls State Park

41382 W. M-123, Paradise 49768, 906-492-3415
michigan.gov/dnr

CHECK PHOTO OP WITH BEAR CUB
OFF YOUR BUCKET LIST

For the love of black bears, in 1997 Dean and Jewel Oswald developed a rescue operation for orphaned cubs that also serves as a rehab facility for injured bears. At Oswald's Bear Ranch, visitors follow paths and climb raised platforms to view and photograph bears at home in spacious (and fenced) habitats. The all-bear sanctuary, on 240 acres southwest of Tahquamenon Falls, is the largest of its kind in the United States, and usually houses about 30 to 40 bears. Don't miss the chance to have your photo taken with a black bear cub.

13814 County Rd. 407, Newberry 49868, 906-293-3147
oswaldsbearranch.com
Seasonal

25

GHOST HUNT
AT THE CALUMET THEATRE

The population of the Keweenaw Peninsula exploded with the nineteenth-century copper boom, and in 1900 the Calumet community decided to build an opera house, one of the first municipal theaters in the country. Stars of the era found their way to the stage of the ornate Calumet Theatre, including Douglas Fairbanks Sr., Lillian Russell, Lon Chaney Sr., Sarah Bernhardt, John Phillip Sousa, and Madame Helena Modjeska. In 1958, some 50 years after she died, the story is told that Modjeska returned to the Calumet stage to assist an actress who had forgotten a line. In the years since, many ghostly encounters with the actress have been reported. Restored to its gold, crimson, and ivory splendor, the 700-seat theatre hosts a mix of plays, musicals, films, and concerts. Guided tours are available, ghost sightings not guaranteed.

340 6th St., Calumet 49913, 906-337-2610
calumettheatre.com

REFLECT ON LIFE
AT THE MIRROR OF HEAVEN

A short, wooded trail opens to the jaw-dropping sight of Kitch-iti-kipi, the Big Spring, and its crystal-clear water in jewel-like shades of green. The surrounding forest is perfectly reflected in the 200-foot-wide pond that the Chippewa called "Mirror of Heaven." Ride a self-propelled, cable-guided raft with viewing wells across the 40-foot-deep spring, where 10,000 gallons of water per minute bubble up from the limestone below. Submerged mossy tree trunks, giant brown trout, and changing shapes of sand appear eerie and unfamiliar. Because the water remains at 45 degrees and never freezes, the Big Spring at Palms Book State Park can be viewed year-round.

On M-149, eight miles north of US-2, west of Manistique, 906-341-2355
Search Palms Book State Park at michigan.gov/dnr

27

THINK LIKE AN AGATE
FOR ROCKIN' SUCCESS

Lake Superior's shore is prime territory for rock pickers, whether looking for prized agates or just pretty rocks. Serious rock hounds know that Grand Marais, a fishing village at the eastern gateway to Pictured Rocks National Lakeshore, is a prime hunting ground for agates. It's also home to the Gitche Gumee Agate and History Museum owned by Karen Brzys, aka The Agate Lady. An expert on the semi-precious gemstone who has written books on the subject, she conducts private classes to help novices learn to identify rocks and "think like an agate" for rock hounding success. She believes that whether you take home agates or add to an "oh, how pretty!" collection, meditative time spent staring at rocks next to the big lake is time well spent.

E21739 Brazel St., Grand Marais 49839, 906-494-3000
agatelady.com

TIP

Visit the A.E. Seaman Mineral Museum at Michigan Tech University to see the definitive collection of Michigan minerals and extensive collections from the Great Lakes region and elsewhere.

1404 E. Sharon Ave., Houghton 49931, 906-487-2572
museum.mtu.edu

WING IT
IN PARADISE

It doesn't take an experienced birder to appreciate the sight of the raptor migration at Whitefish Point, north of Paradise on Lake Superior. The tapered Whitefish promontory protrudes toward Canada, forming a funnel attractive to tens of thousands of peregrine falcons, golden and bald eagles, and Cooper's and other hawks during their spring and fall journeys. More than 340 species of birds have been recorded at Whitefish Point, which is one of 14 Eastern UP locations, including Seney National Wildlife Refuge and Tahquamenon Falls State Park, on the Superior Birding Trail described in a map and brochure available on the trail website.

superiorbirdingtrail.com

TIP

For birding locations across the UP, search birding at uptravel.com

SPEND A FREE DAY
AT THE BEACH

Life is short, and so is beach season in the UP; some say that day goes by way too fast. (Yooper humor.) With 1,700 miles of Great Lakes coastline, there's no shortage of beaches—dozens of them free to enjoy and within easy reach, right along the UP's two east-west highways. West of St. Ignace, US-2 follows miles of Lake Michigan sand and a string of beaches that invite a stroll or swim in the shallow waters. Au Train Beach on Lake Superior is one of a series of roadside parks that dot the stretch of M-28 between Munising and Marquette. For a bit more adventure, head out on the two-lane northeast of L'Anse to the remote, best-kept-secret beach at the mouth of the Huron River on the edge of the Huron Mountain Wilderness.

TIP

The Baraga County Travel Guide has a map to the mouth of the Huron River; find it at baragacounty.org

FIND A MOOSE
ON THE LOOSE

Moose are a big deal in the UP. Well, they're a big deal anywhere they roam. The mammals are the largest members of the deer family, measuring up to nine feet tall and weighing as much as 1,200 pounds. Plus, they have sizeable antlers. Newberry has declared itself the official "Moose Capital" of Michigan, claiming that most sightings happen in and around Tahquamenon Falls State Park. However, of the 533 moose that the DNR estimates live in the UP (not including those on Isle Royale National Park), fewer than 100 call the Newberry area home; the rest are near Van Riper State Park, west of Marquette. Chances of a casual moose sighting are improved in areas where they forage at dawn and dusk, near watering holes, and in grazing fields.

Newberry Area Tourism Association
906-293-5562
newberrytourism.com

Van Riper State Park
851 County Rd. AKE, Champion 49814, 906-339-4461
michigan.gov/dnr

TIP

These animals are not friendly and can be very dangerous. Never approach a moose. If you're on a photo safari, bring a very long camera lens.

GET A BROCKWAY MOUNTAIN HIGH

The anticipation builds as you leave Eagle Harbor, following the two-lane road built by Depression era work project crews in 1933. Brockway Mountain Drive makes a slow ascent as it winds toward the tip of the Keweenaw Peninsula. At the summit, soak in expansive views of Lake Superior—and perhaps a passing freighter—more than 700 feet below. All around there are woods and rocky cliffs. In fall, the patchwork of colors is spectacular. Sunsets over the water are breathtaking. On the descent, as the road heads northward to Copper Harbor, pull off for a view of the village and Gitche Gumee below. The impressions made in less than 10 miles will last a lifetime.

Search Brockway Mountain Drive at uptravel.com

PICK A WOODTICK
OR OTHER MUSIC FEST

Woodtick Music Festival legend has it that in 1994, the invitation went out for a few buddies to get together, "cook some hot dogs and watch the Packers . . . and bring your guitar." It exploded into a jam session someone dubbed "a little Woodstock," which in a Yooper's mind went straight to "Woodtick," after the bloodsucking pest common to the northwoods. The Woodtick Music Festival has been held ever since. Music festivals happen throughout the summer across the UP, including those listed on the following page.

Grand Marais Music and Arts Festival
American roots, folk, rock, jazz, bluegrass

August, Grand Marais
906-494-2447
grandmaraismichigan.com

Hiawatha Traditional Music Festival
Celtic, bluegrass, folk music, and traditional dance

July, Marquette Tourist Park
906-226-8575
hiawathamusic.org

Pine Mountain Music Festival
Opera, classical, jazz, blues

June-July, multiple Western UP venues
906-482-1542
pmmf.org

Porcupine Mountains Music Festival
Folk, blues, contemporary

August, Winter Sports Complex
Porcupine Mountains Wilderness State Park, Ontonagon
906-231-1589
porkiesfestival.org

Woodtick Music Festival
Bluegrass, country, rock, blues, folk

August, Hermansville
906-498-2223
woodtickfestival.com

33

CHILL OUT
AT EBEN ICE CAVES

The Eben Ice Caves are not actually caves but vertical sheets of ice that form when seeping water and melting snow drip over rock outcrops. The liquid freezes to form ice curtains, typically with cavities or hollows that allow entry and exploration. No ice climbing experience is needed to enjoy the giant icicle formations, but cleats on boots are strongly suggested to help with footing on the slippery ground surface. This is not a drive-up-hop-out-of-the-car-for-a-quick-peek excursion. The ice caves are located in the Rock River Canyon Wilderness, in the Hiawatha National Forest north of Eben Junction. Parking is in a field, about a mile trail hike away from the ice caves. Don't forget the camera!

The Eben Ice Caves location, between Marquette and Munising, is tricky to find. For detailed directions, go to munising.org

TIP

Monitor weather conditions that might affect the stability and safety of the ice caves; temperature changes can cause melting and the risk of falling ice.

SLOW DOWN, WAY DOWN
IN THE TAHQUAMENON WILDERNESS

If you've got a day to while away, hop aboard the Tahquamenon Falls Wilderness Excursion for a one-of-a-kind trip that combines a narrow-gauge train ride through the forest, a Tahquamenon riverboat cruise, and half-mile hike to a special view of the tannin-colored Upper Falls. The day trips date to 1927, when an entrepreneur transformed a logged-out tract of land and abandoned railroad spur into a tourist attraction. The entire outing lasts six and a half hours; food, beverages, and restrooms are available on the double-decker riverboat. If you have less than two hours to spare, take just the Toonerville Trolley train ride and be on the lookout for deer, bear, moose, and other local animal species alongside the track.

7195 C.R. 381, Soo Junction, 888-778-7246 or 906-876-2311
trainandboattours.com
Seasonal

35

SAIL AWAY
ON THE GREAT LAKES

There's no better way to appreciate the vast freshwater seas than to get out on the water to experience their winds, waves, and moods. You can board a tour boat cruising through the Soo Locks or along the Pictured Rocks shoreline, or charter a fishing service that operates on Lakes Huron, Michigan, or Superior. Mackinac Island ferries make scheduled lighthouse, sunset, and fireworks cruises through the Straits of Mackinac and beyond. But there's nothing like the thrill of slicing powerfully through the formidable Lake Superior under the billowing sails of a nineteenth-century vessel. Superior Odyssey's *Coaster II*, a 58-foot, two-masted coasting schooner built in 1933, departs Marquette's Lower Harbor on two-, four-, and eight-hour charter outings.

Superior Odyssey *Coaster II*

Lake Superior, Marquette, 906-361-3668
superiorodyssey.com

Shepler's Ferry Lighthouse Cruises
Straits of Mackinac
Several cruises pass 11 lights along different routes

800-828-6157
sheplersferry.com

Star Line Mackinac Island Ferry
Straits of Mackinac
Evening cruises catch the Lake Michigan sunset from under the Mackinac Bridge, and fireworks displays on late summer Saturdays

800-638-9892 or 906-643-7635
mackinacferry.com

Search charter fishing at uptravel.com

FORAGE
FOR FREE FOOD

The fields and woods of the UP yield a bounty of wild foods, and foraging for blueberries, raspberries, strawberries, thimbleberries, mushrooms, leeks, and other edible plants is a fun pastime that yields a tangible benefit: free eats! Equipment needs are minimal and all ages can participate, but study up on what foods are safe to consume (it's vital to know the difference between morels and a similar-looking poisonous mushroom). Ask around for tips on where to hunt; you may find a generous Yooper willing to share secret patches. On state park land in the UP, you're free to hand-gather edible foods. Rare or endangered plants are off limits.

TIP

Seney National Wildlife Refuge, a 95,000-acre sanctuary for birds and wildlife in the Eastern UP, permits picking of its many berry and mushroom varieties.

1674 Refuge Entrance Rd., Seney 49883, 906-586-9851
fws.gov/refuge/seney/

STOP AND SMELL THE LILACS
ON MACKINAC ISLAND

The fragrance of lilacs fills the Mackinac Island air each June as the flowering trees—some of which arrived at Mackinac before the Civil War—blossom in various shades of purple, pink, violet, white, and even yellow. Conditions are right for three species to thrive on the island, including 100 varieties of the Common Lilac. The Mackinac Island Lilac Festival began in 1949 as a one-day celebration of the blooms and has evolved into the island's largest event. Each June, it's a feast for all senses, with concerts, beer, wine and food tastings, 10k run, lectures, walking tours with a lilac expert, and closing with the lovely Lilac Festival Grand Parade, featuring our fair Lilac Queen.

906-847-3783
mackinacisland.org

ROUND UP THE POSSE

FOR THE UP PRO RODEO

Cowboys and cowgirls have been heading to Iron River since 1968 for the UP Championship Rodeo and a hot summer weekend of bull riding, roping, steer wrestling, team roping, barrel racing, and saddle bronc and bareback riding. There's family-friendly fun with activities for the kids, a craft show, fun runs, Miss UP Rodeo horsemanship competition, coronation of the Rodeo Queen, pancake and chuck wagon breakfasts, and Saturday morning's Wild West Parade. The rodeo at the Iron County Fairgrounds is sanctioned by the Professional Rodeo Cowboys Association.

720 W. Franklin St., Iron River 49935, 906-284-9680
upprorodeo.com

BE DAZZLED
BY THE NORTHERN LIGHTS

There are no guarantees in life or northern lights, but chances of catching the colorful sky displays are above average in the UP, due to a combination of latitude, dark skies, and wide open spaces. Auroras borealis sometimes occur overhead, but more often the swirling, shimmering dances are low in the sky. A spot on a Great Lakes shore with unobstructed views of the horizon, preferably along Lake Superior looking northward, is ideal. Prime northern lights viewing season is between August and April; peak months are October, November, and April, when the nights are cold and crisp. Despite many online sources for predicting, tracking, and real-time sharing of aurora sightings, they're still unpredictable. It's best to prepare for the possibility, hope for the best, and—if nothing else—enjoy the Milky Way, meteor shower, or whatever show the sky delivers that evening.

Search northern lights at uptravel.com

40

TAKE A PEEK
FROM THE PEAK

Named for exploratory mine pits on its site near Ironwood, Copper Peak is the world's largest artificial ski jump, and in 1970 hosted the first international ski flying competition. As Copper Peak Adventure Ride, it delivers adrenaline-rushing thrills that begin with an 810-foot chairlift ride to an elevator, which travels 18 stories to an observation deck. From there, an eight-story stair climb leads to the very top and an unobstructed, 40-mile view of the Porcupine Mountains, Lake Superior, and endless forests that are especially stunning in autumn colors.

N13870 Copper Peak Rd., Ironwood 49938, 906-932-3500
copperpeak.com
Seasonal

41

JUST BREATHE

Northern Michigan's tourism industry dates back to the late 1800s, when summers in cities were dreadful: the hot air choked with foul odors and the sky darkened by pollution. Steamship companies and railroads saw a market and promoted an escape to the fresh air and clean water found at distant hotels and resorts (which, conveniently, the transportation companies had constructed). Urbanites with the means to travel packed their trunks and headed north to revel in the healthy environment. The sales tactic continued into the 1930s, when UP promotional brochures promised tourists they'd enjoy "Happy, Carefree Days and Restful Nights . . . scenic beauty . . . clean air . . . No Hay Fever!" Wherever you travel in the UP, just breathe, and decide whether you agree that the air really is cleaner, clearer, and undefinably different than anywhere else.

IVERSON

SPORTS AND RECREATION

PLAY
IN YOUR PLUS FOURS

A horse-drawn taxi carries you to Mackinac Island's Wawashkamo Golf Club, which occupies the site of the Battle of 1814, the Americans' failed attempt to retake the island from the British. The nine-hole, links-style course, with natural hazards and fairways defined by mowed grass, remains essentially unchanged since Scotsman Alex Smith designed it in 1898. Each summer Wawashkamo (the name means "walk a crooked trail") hosts the National Hickory Stick Tournament. If this isn't the course for vintage golf garb, what is? Perhaps The Jewel, Grand Hotel's course in two parts. The first nine holes were built adjacent to the resort in 1901 and redesigned in 1987 by Jerry Matthews. He also laid out the second nine holes, a carriage ride and a century away.

Wawashkamo Golf Club
British Landing Rd., Mackinac Island 49757, 906-847-3871
wawashkamo.com

The Jewel
Grand Ave., Mackinac Island 49757, 906-847-9218
grandhotel.com

Among the UP's 50 public golf courses, Greywalls in Marquette earns raves for the challenging 18 holes that Mike DeVries designed around natural granite outcroppings, a trout stream, wetlands, rock walls, and views of Lake Superior (with occasional winds off the water).

1075 Grove St., Marquette 49855, 906-225-0721
marquettegolfclub.com

CAMP THE YOOP
YOUR WAY

Roughing it is relative, and camping comfort is measured in degrees. Hankering to haul most of your worldly goods with you in an RV with satellite TV? Modern UP campgrounds can hook you up. Prefer to pack your pup tent into the backcountry? The UP has wilderness. Short on gear? No fear: some state parks rent rustic cabins, utilitarian yurts, and well-equipped lodges. Whatever your preference, spend at least a couple of days and nights exploring the great outdoors, toasting marshmallows, telling scary stories around a campfire, and sleeping under the stars.

Search campgrounds at uptravel.com

Michigan State Parks require a Recreation Passport (daily or annual) for entry. For information and camping reservations, go to michigan.gov/dnr.

TIP

Leave the campfire wood behind, and buy it where you burn it.
To prevent spread of forest pests and diseases,
no firewood may be carried into the UP.

FOR A RUSH,
GO MUSH

Thrill to the beauty of swooshing through snow-covered wilderness, your sled pulled by a team of huskies flying to the sound of silence. Nature's Kennel Sled Dog Racing & Adventures is one of several UP outfits that will take you for a ride or teach you to mush with your own team. On half- or full-day outings, or overnight excursions, you'll learn to care for and talk to your team (hint: commands do not include "mush"). Children may ride along; kids 10 and older can learn to drive. With Nature's Kennel, you can even race in a noncompetitive event during the Tahquamenon Country Sled Dog Race, held each January at Muskallonge Lake State Park. The Tahquamenon races, like February's UP200 in Marquette, and Calumet's CopperDog 150 in March, are festive events for mobs of bundled-up spectators, too.

Nature's Kennel Sled Dog Racing & Adventures
14785 North CR 415, McMillan 49853, 906-748-0513
natureskennel.com

CopperDog 150, Calumet
copperdog150.com

Tahquamenon Country Sled Dog Race, Newberry
tcsdr.org

UP200, Marquette
up200.org

PICTURE YOURSELF
AT THE NATIONAL LAKESHORE

Sculpted and painted by nature, the multi-colored, mineral-stained sandstone cliffs that tower 200 feet above Lake Superior give Pictured Rocks National Lakeshore its name. The park's shoreline stretches 42 miles, from the western gateway at Munising eastward to Grand Marais. With beaches, dunes, waterfalls, inland lakes, streams, and thick forests, its 73,000 acres are a year-round playground for silent sports enthusiasts. The trail system has short, accessible paths to scenic overlooks as well as strenuous wilderness hikes, and there is rustic and primitive backcountry camping. Lake Superior's unpredictable nature can challenge even expert sea kayakers; guided kayak outings are an option. A Pictured Rocks Cruise is the most leisurely way to enjoy the scenery. For views with a thrill, choose the speed and spins of the jet-propelled Riptide Ride: it rocks.

TIP

Be prepared for Lake Superior's changeable weather by dressing in layers. Pack bug dope in warm weather months.

Pictured Rocks National Lakeshore

906-387-3700
nps.gov/piro

Munising Visitors Bureau

906-387-1717
munising.org

Grand Marais Visitor Info

906-494-2447
grandmaraismichigan.com

Pictured Rocks Cruises

100 City Park Dr., Munising 49862, 906-387-2379
picturedrocks.com

Riptide Ride

1309 Commercial St., Munising 49862, 906-387-8888
riptideride.com

46

LUGE YOURSELF
AT LUCY HILL

Slide like an Olympian at the naturbahn luge in Negaunee, the only full-length natural luge track in the United States. Athletes-in-training reach speeds of up to 50 miles per hour on the winding, half-mile course. The lower portion of the naturally snow-packed and icy track is open to the public on weekends (weather permitting), December through March. You'll learn to control the naturbahn luge sled with your feet, hands, and body to follow the hill's natural contours. Gear—helmet, sled, and braking shoes—is provided by the Upper Peninsula Luge Club, which has produced a number of Olympic sliders.

230 E. County Rd., Negaunee 49866, 906-250-1813
upluge.org

TREK THE PORKIES

Lake Superior washes up against more than 20 miles of Porcupine Mountains Wilderness State Park shoreline in the Western UP. "The Porkies," at nearly 60,000 acres, make up Michigan's largest state park and deliver both backcountry challenges and family-friendly adventures, from mountain biking, skiing, and hunting to fishing and rustic cabin camping. Make the Visitor Center your first stop for an update on trail conditions, wildlife sightings, and free hands-on programs. Guided nature hikes whet the appetite for exploring 90 miles of trails through old-growth forest and along rivers to waterfalls. Hike to Summit Peak, the park's highest point at just under 2,000 feet, for sweeping views from a wooden observation tower. The more challenging, four-mile Escarpment Trail has a backcountry feel. Or take a short walk to an ADA-accessible overlook for spectacular views of the ethereal Lake of the Clouds.

Porcupine Mountains Visitor Center
33303 Headquarters Rd., Ontonagon 49953, 906-885-5275
michigan.gov/porkiesvc

TIP

The Porkies are home to black bears, and sightings are common. Know before you go or ask at the Visitor Center for tips on handling bear encounters.

48

GO FOR THE BIG SNOW

With more than 200 inches of average annual snowfall, the Western UP has earned the nickname Big Snow Country. It's home to several downhill ski areas and resorts, along with Porcupine Mountains Wilderness State Park, which has a 641-foot vertical drop. Expert skiers and snowboarders head to Mt. Bohemia's vertical drop of 900 feet and extreme backcountry territory on the east coast of the Keweenaw Peninsula, where each season the snowfall approaches 300 inches. At lower elevations, there are hundreds of miles of trails throughout the area for classic and skate-style cross-country skiing, rated novice to expert. Annual XC ski events include the Great Bear Chase marathon in Calumet and the Noquemanon Ski Marathon in Marquette.

For ski and snowboard areas and resorts, and XC ski trails and events, search winter activities at uptravel.com

Mt. Bohemia
6532 Lac La Belle Rd., Lac La Belle 49950, 906-289-4105
mtbohemia.com

Great Bear Chase Ski Marathon
greatbearchase.com

Noquemanon Ski Marathon
noquemanon.com

TIP

The National Skiing Association was founded in Ishpeming, known as the "Birthplace of Organized Skiing." Visit the US Ski & Snowboard Hall of Fame and Museum, and take a selfie with the 22-foot statue of a ski jumper out front.

610 Palms Ave. (US-41), Ishpeming 49849, 906-485-6323
skihall.com

PADDLE YOUR OWN CANOE (OR KAYAK OR SUP)

Paddling is a three-season sport in the UP, where you're never farther than six miles from a stream, river, or lake—inland or the Great Lakes Huron, Michigan, and Superior. By canoe, kayak, raft, or stand-up paddle board, you can choose a guided trip, a gentle and family-friendly outing, a strenuous excursion into backcountry, a state or national park waterway, an adrenaline-pumping white water adventure, a romantic moonlit paddle, or a challenging Great Lakes coastline tour along one of seven UP Water Trails. Rentals and guided excursions are plentiful. Waterside lodging and campgrounds are plentiful. Scenery and wildlife sightings are plentiful. Water you waiting for?

Michigan Water Trails: michiganwatertrails.org

Search paddle sports at michigan.org

SKATE

WHERE PRO HOCKEY WAS BORN

Houghton became the "Birthplace of Organized Professional Ice Hockey" in 1904 when James Dee and John "Doc" Gibson formed the International Hockey League. They initiated regular paychecks to players, lifting amateurs to pro status. Check out the History of Hockey exhibit, and bring skates for open ice and hockey sessions at Dee Stadium. Or head to St. Ignace in February, when 30 ice rinks on Lake Huron's Moran Bay host 200 teams in the UP Pond Hockey Championship.

birthplaceofprohockey.org

Dee Stadium
700 E. Lakeshore Dr., Houghton 49931, 906-482-7760
cityofhoughton.com/rec-dee.php

UP Pond Hockey
800-338-6660
stignace.com

REV UP
FOR A SNOWMOBILE RIDE

With 3,300 miles of designated snowmobile trails and average annual snowfall of 60 to 240 inches, sledheads agree with industry magazines that rate the UP tops in scenery and overall best snowmobiling and describe the western end as an "epic snowmobile destination." There are plenty of sled-friendly places for trailside gas, supplies, food, and lodging, and at its website, the Michigan Snowmobile Association lists a dozen outlets for rental sleds and gear in the 906 area code. Varied terrain at state and national parks and national forests satisfies families, beginners, and extreme sledders who hit wilderness trails and cross open fields to stunning views of the Great Lakes, waterfalls, ice caves, frozen inland lakes, challenging backcountry, and ice bridges to islands. Registration and trail permits are required and available online, where there are trail maps and links to trail reports.

Search snowmobile at michigan.gov/dnr

Search snowmobile at uptravel.com

Michigan Snowmobile Association: msasnow.org

See drivers tackle an icy, one-mile oval at speeds of up to 115 mph at the International 500 Snowmobile Race in Sault Ste. Marie. The nation's oldest, biggest snowmobile race is held in early February.

984 W. 4th Ave., Sault Ste. Marie 49783, 906-635-1500
i-500.com

TAKE A TIP
FROM THE SNOWSHOE PRIEST

Knee-deep snow is no problem when you strap on snowshoes to walk atop the white stuff. Bishop Frederic Baraga depended on them during the mid-1800s to reach far-flung missions throughout the long UP winters. A gigantic bronze likeness of the beloved Snowshoe Priest, clutching a seven-foot cross and 26-foot-long snowshoes, overlooks Keweenaw Bay near L'Anse. Native Americans developed the ancient form of winter transportation, now popular with snowshoe trekkers of all ages who blaze trails through forests, along beaches, and across wilderness acres to remote and quiet beauty spots at state and national parks, recreation areas, and wildlife sanctuaries. Snowshoe rentals are available at several outfitters across the UP.

For snowshoe trails, search winter activities at uptravel.com

TIP

Trails are lantern-lit on select Saturday evenings for snowshoe hikes at a handful of state parks including Mackinac Island, Porcupine Mountains and Tahquamenon Falls.

Michigan.gov/dnr

HUNT, FISH, TRAP, BRAG

"It's like Christmas with guns," is how a Yooper describes deer camp in *Escanaba in da Moonlight*, a wacky film by Michigan native Jeff Daniels. Hunting, fishing, and trapping have been the fabric of life in the UP since Native Americans subsisted on its bounty of fish, fowl, and large and small game. European voyageurs and trappers built a booming trade on its furs. Nineteenth-century moguls made great tracts of the UP their private sporting retreats, and Ernest Hemingway wrote about fly fishing the Fox River (which he renamed for his short story "Big Two-Hearted River"). Ice shanty villages pop up each winter, and charter captains share their secrets of the freshwater seas. Guides and outfitters are ready to help novice and veteran hunters make the most out of the four-season, outdoor experience that is a way of life across the UP.

Michigan Department of Natural Resources
517-284-6057
michigan.gov/dnr

TIP

Required hunting, fishing, and trapping licenses and applications, as well as regulations and maps of land and water open to the public are available online at michigan.gov/dnr.

GO TO EXTREMES
ON LAND, SEA, AND ICE

The rugged terrain and inland seas afford extreme adventurers a mix of opportunities and a variety of extreme sports, especially in the Western UP and Keweenaw Peninsula:

Mountain and fat-tire bikers find designated trails plus countless miles of old logging roads and railroad grades to explore. Check out the Noquemanon Trails Network's Snow Bike Route in Marquette and the Copper Harbor Mountain Bike Trails. Rent bikes and get guidance at Keweenaw Adventure Company in Copper Harbor. keweenawadventure.com

Lake Superior's best surfing (yes, like with a wet suit on a surfboard) is from October through March in Marquette and on the Keweenaw Peninsula. Find surfing gear and tips at Downwind Sports. downwindsports.com

An abundance of frozen waterfalls and water seeping from sandstone bluffs make the UP a prime ice climbing destination. The "ice monkeys" at Downwind Sports can tip you off to dozens of climbs—and provide rental gear. downwindsports.com

TIP

The annual Michigan Ice Fest is packed with clinics, classes, demonstrations, and, of course, climbing in the Munising area.

michiganicefest.com

MARCH TO A DIFFERENT DRUMMOND

It's just a 10-minute car ferry ride between DeTour Village and Drummond Island across the St. Marys River, the US-Canada border at the eastern end of the UP. But Drummond, the second largest island in the Great Lakes, feels a world away. Its 150-mile Lake Huron shoreline is a series of coves and islands to explore by paddle power, and to dive on shipwrecks. More than half of Drummond's 87,000 acres are state owned, and its interior has 34 lakes, thick woods, marshes, and meadows to fish, hunt, boat, hike, camp, off-road, snowmobile, and cross-country ski. Drummond also provides nature lovers with plenty of places to spy wildflowers, birds, and wildlife. Look no further than its geographic features, like the Marble Head Cliffs, the Fossil Ledges, giant puddingstones, and rare Maxton Plains alvar landscape to see what makes Drummond different.

Drummond Island Tourism Association
906-493-5245 or 800-737-8666
drummondislandchamber.com

GET OFF THE BEATEN PATH
ON ORV TRAILS

Head out for a ride to remember on three-season trails designated for ATVs, ORVs, and motorcycles. As a bonus in the UP, off-roaders can also travel the extensive network of state forest roads. Rugged areas like Michigan's most remote state park at Craig Lake, in the Western UP, are best accessed by Jeeps, 4x4s, and other SUVs. At the eastern tip of the peninsula, it's a short ferry ride to Drummond Island and the 117-mile, closed-loop ATV/ORV trail that traverses ancient forests and provides memorable off-road experiences, including the rocky Steps at Marble Head. Be sure to get an ORV license and permit, available online at the DNR site. Need wheels? Rentals are plentiful across the UP.

Search trails at uptravel.com

Search ORV/ATV at michigan.gov/dnr for trail maps, rules, and permit and license information.

TIP
Pick up paper maps that detail county and seasonal roads for whatever area you're exploring. GPS is not reliable in these parts, and cell service isn't always available.

DIVE INTO MARITIME HISTORY
AT AN UNDERWATER PRESERVE

The Great Lakes were Michigan's first highways and are the final resting place for thousands of vessels that succumbed to storms, treacherous waters, flawed equipment, and human error. Recreational scuba divers and snorkelers explore schooners, steamers, barges, and freighters preserved in cold fresh waters at depths as shallow as five feet. Sea caves and other geological formations are a bonus at some locations. More than 100 sites are in the protected UP waters of the Alger, DeTour Passage, Keweenaw, Marquette, Straits of Mackinac, and Whitefish Point Underwater Preserves, as well as at Isle Royale National Park. Strict laws forbid removal of artifacts (it's a felony), so there's a rich inventory of relics at many of the wrecks. Divers need drysuits to protect from temperatures of 40° F and below.

Michigan Underwater Preserves
800-970-8717
mupc.net

Isle Royale National Park
906-482-0984
nps.gov/isro

Non-divers can see two wrecks from the comfort of the two-hour Glass Bottom Shipwreck Tour in Munising Bay.

1204 Commercial St., Munising 49862, 906-387-4477
shipwrecktours.com

JUMP OFF A CLIFF
AT BLACK ROCKS

Rocky obstacles and frigid waters be danged, cliff diving is an irresistible challenge for adrenaline junkies who are not deterred by the chilling waters of Lake Superior. At the billion-year-old Black Rocks at Marquette's Presque Isle Park, taking a 10- to 15-foot leap into the deep, cold Gitche Gumee is a long-standing tradition and rite of passage for generations of Yoopers. The water is usually warmest in August, but jumpers climb out onto the rocks throughout the season. The Black Rocks are just one of the beauty spots on Presque Isle, a 323-acre city treasure with walking and biking trails, picnic areas, and a prime spot to watch the sun set.

906-228-0460
mqtcty.org/parks-presque-isle.php

HIKE
THROUGH A CATHEDRAL OF TREES

The UP has trails for gentle hikes and strenuous backcountry hikes. Accessible trails. Trails that lead to waterfalls and to expansive vistas. Trails that connect to other trails. And trails that transport you to another era. A hike at Estivant Pines Nature Sanctuary near Copper Harbor takes you back 500 years, to the time before aggressive logging operations nearly depleted Michigan's forests. Through a citizen-led effort, this 510-acre tract protects one of the last stands of old-growth white pine in the state. Two trails, each about a mile, connect to form a loop through the woods where pines reach 125 feet toward the heavens. This sanctuary near the tip of the Keweenaw Peninsula is home to 85 bird species, native orchids, wildflowers, and ferns, as well as Michigan's official state tree, the white pine.

Burma Rd., Copper Harbor
866-223-2231
michigannature.org

TIP

On any hike, bring bug dope.

GO WILD
FOR ISLE ROYALE

Rugged and remote Isle Royale is one of the least-visited National Parks in the system, and that's just fine with solitude-seeking backpackers, hikers, paddlers, anglers, photographers, and shipwreck divers. The 400-island Lake Superior archipelago, 55 miles from the Keweenaw Peninsula, is accessible only by boat or seaplane from mid-April through October. Rock Harbor is the park's hub of activity, with lodging, a restaurant, snack bar, store, boat rentals, and ranger-led programs. But most adventurers head to the 165 miles of wilderness hiking trails for awe-inspiring scenery and wildlife sightings that might include moose. The 45-mile-long island, dotted with primitive campsites, has strict guidelines in place to balance human access with protection of the ancient ecosystem, recognized as a Biosphere Reserve.

906-482-0984
nps.gov/isro

TIP

Be prepared for potentially rough seas on the three- and six-hour ferry rides from Copper Harbor and Houghton. There's also a ferry from Grand Portage, MN, and seaplane from Houghton. Private boats and seaplanes are allowed.

PLAY IT COOL
IN THE SNOWS

Les Cheneaux (French for "the channels," pronounced LAY-shen-O), nicknamed "The Snows" by locals, is a glacier-formed archipelago of 36 islands in the Mackinac Straits of the Eastern UP. A summertime vacation area since the late 1800s, it has a throwback, low-key vibe that makes the 12-mile stretch of Lake Huron shore a cool place to chill out. Poke around the shops and museums in the mainland towns of Hessel and Cedarville, drop a fishing line off a wooden dock, and catch the sunrise from a waterfront cottage. An annual festival honors conservationist Aldo Leopold, the "father of wildlife ecology," who spent summers of his youth exploring Les Cheneaux. Join a guided excursion by Woods & Water Ecotours to understand why The Nature Conservancy named this one of the Western Hemisphere's "Last Great Places."

680 W. M-134, Cedarville 49719, 888-364-7526
lescheneaux.org

Woods & Water Ecotours
20 S. Pickford Ave., Hessel 49745, 906-484-4157
upecotours.com

TIP

Boats have always been the main means of traveling Les Cheneaux, and the large number of vintage watercraft still in use inspired the Antique Wooden Boat Show & Festival of Arts, a showcase of classic beauties in Hessel's marina each August.

906-484-2821
lciboatshow.com

CULTURE AND HISTORY

CROSS THAT BRIDGE
WHEN YOU COME TO IT

Construction of the Brooklyn Bridge in 1883 inspired Michigan visionaries who imagined a similar link between the state's two landmasses. But it wasn't until 1957 when the five-mile Mackinac Bridge replaced ferries that had been the only connection between Mackinaw City in the Lower Peninsula and St. Ignace in the UP. Spanning the Straits of Mackinac, where the Great Lakes Huron and Michigan meet, the graceful, twin-towered "Mighty Mac" suspension bridge is an engineering marvel, with spectacular views of islands, the deep and color-changing waters, ferries, and the occasional freighter. If you're not crazy about crossing what Mackinac Bridge designer Dr. David B. Steinman called "a poem in steel," leave the driving to a Bridge Authority employee who will take the wheel of your vehicle. The free service is available 24/7 by calling 906-643-7600.

906-643-7600
mackinacbridge.org

TIP

The annual Labor Day Bridge Walk is your chance to join 45,000 pedestrians who stroll from St. Ignace to Mackinaw City in two lanes closed to traffic. At all other times, hikers (as well as snowmobilers and bicyclists) can pay a fee to hitch a ride with the bridge transport service. mackinacbridge.org

MIGHTY MAC STATS

Passenger vehicle toll is $4 (cash only); RV and truck tolls are higher

Length of bridge: 26,372 feet

Height of twin towers above water: 552 feet

Roadway width: 54 feet

Height of roadway above water at midspan: 199 feet

Depth of water below bridge: up to 295 feet

Length of wire in main cables: 42,000 miles

Diameter of main cables: 24.5 inches

Weight of bridge: 1,024,500 tons

Number of rivets: 4,851,700

Number of bolts: 1,016,600

Number of workers who built it: 3,500 at site; 7,500 at mills, quarries, shops

Average number of daily crossings: 11,000

BE IN AWE
OF MACKINAC

The history is fascinating, the setting inspiring, and the fudge worth the calories. Mackinac (pronounced Mack-in-awe) is derived from Michilimackinac, the Ojibwa Indian word for "Giant Turtle," the sacred rise of land in the waters where Lakes Huron and Michigan meet. The story of Mackinac Island's evolution into a fur trading center, military outpost, and tourist destination is told in its museums, its pastel nineteenth-century (or replicated) architecture, and the splendid summer homes high above the watery Mackinac Straits. Most visitors arrive by Shepler or Star Line ferry from Mackinaw (yes, it's spelled differently) City in the Lower Peninsula, and St. Ignace in the UP (a local charter airline also provides service). Transportation on the car-free island is by foot, horse-drawn carriage, and bicycle (rental or BYO). With old fashioned activities like pedaling to scenic sites, hiking wooded trails, and playing golf and croquet, it's like a Victorian-era vacation—with selfie sticks.

Mackinac Island Tourism Bureau
906-847-3783
mackinacisland.org

TIP

Mackinac Island, home to about 500 residents, is open year-round. Avoid the crowds and plan a fall color or wintertime visit. Off-season lodging, dining, and services are limited, so plan well ahead.

64

SLEEP LIKE A VICTORIAN
ON MACKINAC ISLAND

A day trip to Mackinac Island is a day to remember, but it takes a night—or several—to fully appreciate the specialness of its car-free, Victorian vibe. Save yourself the mad dash for the last ferry of the day, and relax over dinner, enjoy live music at a pub, stargaze, and wake up to the clip-clopping of horse hooves outside your cozy bed and breakfast, historic hotel, the full-service Mission Point Resort, or the epitome of nineteenth-century resorts—the bluff-top Grand Hotel. Although its nearly 400 rooms and amenities are thoroughly up to date, Grand Hotel maintains traditions such as afternoon tea in the Parlor, croquet on the lawn, dressing for dinner, and orchestra music for dancing. Its 660-foot rocking chair-lined porch invites strolling, sitting, and taking in the views, just as guests have done since 1887.

286 Grand Ave., Mackinac Island 49757, 800-334-7263
grandhotel.com

TIP

The Mackinac Island tourism office has a handy online tool for identifying lodging that suits your needs based on budget, property size, and location, available at mackinacisland.org.

65

GET THE STRAITS STORY
AT THE OJIBWA MUSEUM

On St. Ignace's State Street, amid the bustle of visitors and horn blasts of Mackinac Island ferries, sits the unassuming Museum of Ojibwa Culture, where detailed displays reveal what life was like centuries ago for the first people of the Straits of Mackinac. Housed in a former Catholic church, exhibits describe Ojibwa history before and after the arrival of the Huron and Odawa Indians and French explorers and missionaries. (Don't miss the quality museum shop, which carries only items made by Native Americans.) In adjacent Marquette Mission Park, there's a replica Huron longhouse and the life-size sculptures and descriptive panels of the Anishinaabe Sculpture Park. A statue and the gravesite of Father Jacques Marquette are also on the grounds, which is the site of the St. Ignace mission he established in 1671.

500 N. State St., St. Ignace 49781, 906-643-9161
museumofojibwaculture.net
Seasonal

TIP

Museum special events include Heritage Week and the Native American Festival, which feature traditional dancers, drum circles, and Native food, music, art, and craft demonstrations.

HAVE A BLAST FROM THE PAST
AT UP FORTS

Each Mackinac Island summer day, the boom of a cannon rings out from the whitewashed military outpost on the bluff overlooking the Straits of Mackinac. Civilians ages 13 or older can (for a fee) help a Fort Mackinac soldier load, prime, and fire the first cannon volley of the morning. Costumed interpreters depict life at the 1780 fort, and exhibits in its 14 buildings explain the history of the region. Near the tip of the Keweenaw Peninsula, Fort Wilkins was built in 1844 to keep order in anticipation of conflicts between the Ojibwa Indians and influx of copper miners and prospectors. However, no problems materialized, and the US Army-occupied fort was abandoned in 1846. The original buildings are furnished, and costumed interpreters re-enact daily activities at the isolated post on pretty Lake Fanny Hooe. The forts are open seasonally.

Fort Mackinac
Mackinac Island, 49757
906-847-3328
mackinacparks.com

Fort Wilkins Historic State Park
15223 US-41, Copper Harbor
49918, 906-289-4215
michigan.gov/dnr

TIP

Hike or ride a bike to the highest point on Mackinac Island for a panoramic view of the Straits of Mackinac from the recreated Fort Holmes (origonally built during the war of 1812).

67

LEARN THE LINGO
OF THE YOOP

It's called God's Country, has only one area code (906), and people speak with a vague accent (English with a hint of Canadian-tempered Minnesotan lilt, ala the Coen Brothers' *Fargo*). The UP can seem like a foreign land, so it may help to get grounded by learning some lingo you may encounter in the UP, aka the Yoop:

- Yoopers are natives of the Upper Peninsula (UP-ers)
- Trolls are people who live below Big Mac (Mackinac Bridge)
- "Yes" is "yah," sentences end with "eh" (ay), "th" becomes "d" as in "Say yah to da UP, eh!"
- Sauna, the hot Finnish cleanse, is "SOW-na" (rhymes with cow-na) and may be used without preposition ("We go sauna, eh!").
- Sisu is Finnish for determination, or grit

Don't be surprised if "Holy wah" (whoa!), "jeez oh man" (really?), and "youbetcha" (absolutely) find their way into your vocabulary after a few days in da Yoop, eh?

EAT FLAPJACKS LIKE A LUMBERJACK
AT THE COOK SHACK

Thick woods and lumber camps built Newberry, an Eastern UP logging center established in 1882 on the rail line between Marquette and Sault Ste. Marie. The Tahquamenon Logging Museum just north of town tells the story of the logging industry in a cluster of buildings and equipment displays related to the era when lumber was king. One Saturday morning a month in the summer, a crew of volunteers fires up the wood-burning stove in the log cabin cook shack to rustle up a hearty lumberjack breakfast of pancakes, eggs, sausage, bacon, and potatoes. Flannel shirt not required (but you might consider elastic-waist pants).

On M-123, about a mile north of Newberry, 906-293-3700
loggingmuseum.com
Seasonal

TIP

Check the schedule for traditional music jamborees held two weekends each summer.

GO WITH THE FLOW
IN SAULT STE. MARIE

Any visit to Michigan's oldest city must begin at the St. Marys River, just as it did for Native Americans who gathered there for centuries before 1668, when Father Jacques Marquette named the place Sault Ste. Marie. The River of History Museum traces the origins, people, industries, and life along the waterway that connects Lakes Huron and Superior and separates the United States from Canada (which has its own Sault Ste. Marie). After viewing freighters traveling through the Soo Locks, explore a lake boat that made that passage many times before it was retired to become the Museum Ship Valley Camp. Roam the deck of the 550-foot freighter, step inside the wheelhouse, and study maritime exhibits in the cargo holds. From the 21-story Tower of History, get a view of the Soo Locks, St. Marys River, and beyond.

Sault Ste. Marie Visitor Info
225 E. Portage Ave., Sault Ste. Marie 49783, 800-647-2858
or 906-632-3366
saultstemarie.com

DISCOVER THE PERILS
OF THE SHIPWRECK COAST

On a stormy night in 1975, the ore carrier SS *Edmund Fitzgerald* sank in Lake Superior off Whitefish Point, the critical turning point for freighters entering and leaving the big lake. The treacherous, 80-mile stretch westward is known as the Shipwreck Coast for the number of vessels lost in its dangerous waters. The stories of the sailors and ships are told through exhibits and artifacts at the Great Lakes Shipwreck Museum at Whitefish Point. The tidy compound of white, red-roofed buildings includes the 1861 lighthouse (the oldest operating light on Lake Superior), lighthouse keeper's quarters, and 1923 surf boat house. Although the museum closes for the season at the end of October, it hosts a memorial ceremony each November 10, the date that the *Edmund Fitzgerald* went down with its crew of 29.

18335 N. Whitefish Point Rd., Paradise 49768, 888-492-3747
shipwreckmuseum.com

TIP

Stay overnight in the handsomely restored 1923 Coast Guard Lifeboat Station Crews Quarters. Plan to book a reservation well in advance; the five rooms are in high demand.

NESTLE DOWN
AT A SCANDINAVIAN B&B

Leave your shoes at the door—as is tradition in Sweden and Finland—and enjoy a taste of Scandinavia at the Nestledown Bed & Breakfast in Marquette, where the beds are comfy, the hospitality is warm, and the morning buffet features Finnish foods. The newly built lodging is painted the deep red typical of Nordic wooden structures, with its many windows framed in crisp white, and doors the blue of Lake Superior, just across the road. The inn has five spacious rooms and a suite—each with private bath—plus an apartment above the detached garage. Guests are welcome to relax in the authentic Finnish sauna and two common areas that invite lounging by the fireplace, playing board games, reading, or lingering over a cup of tea and homemade goodies that are set out at 7:30 each evening.

975 N. Lakeshore Blvd., Marquette 49855, 906-273-0996
nestledownmarquette.com

LOCK THROUGH
AT THE SOO

For centuries, Native Americans—and then voyagers, missionaries, and fur traders—portaged their canoes around the St. Marys River rapids to travel between Lakes Superior and Huron at Sault Ste. Marie. But boats got bigger, and the 21-foot difference in water levels became an issue until engineers figured out how to solve that navigational challenge. By 1855 the first substantial Soo Lock was built, followed by increasingly larger locks to accommodate ever-bigger boats. Today's locks use the time-tested system of gates, gravity, and valves that control water depths, lifting and lowering boats to lake levels. Soo Locks Visitor Center displays describe the process, and there's an elevated platform for watching freighters "lock through." You can lock through on a two-hour Soo Locks Boat Tour of the waterway between the United States and Canada, sometimes alongside massive lake and ocean freighters.

Soo Locks Visitor Center
Osborn Blvd., Sault Ste. Marie 49783, 906-253-9290
lre.usace.army.mil/Missions/Recreation/Soo-Locks-Visitor-Center/

Soo Locks Boat Tours
Two dock locations on Portage Ave., Sault Ste. Marie 49783, 800-432-6301
soolocks.com

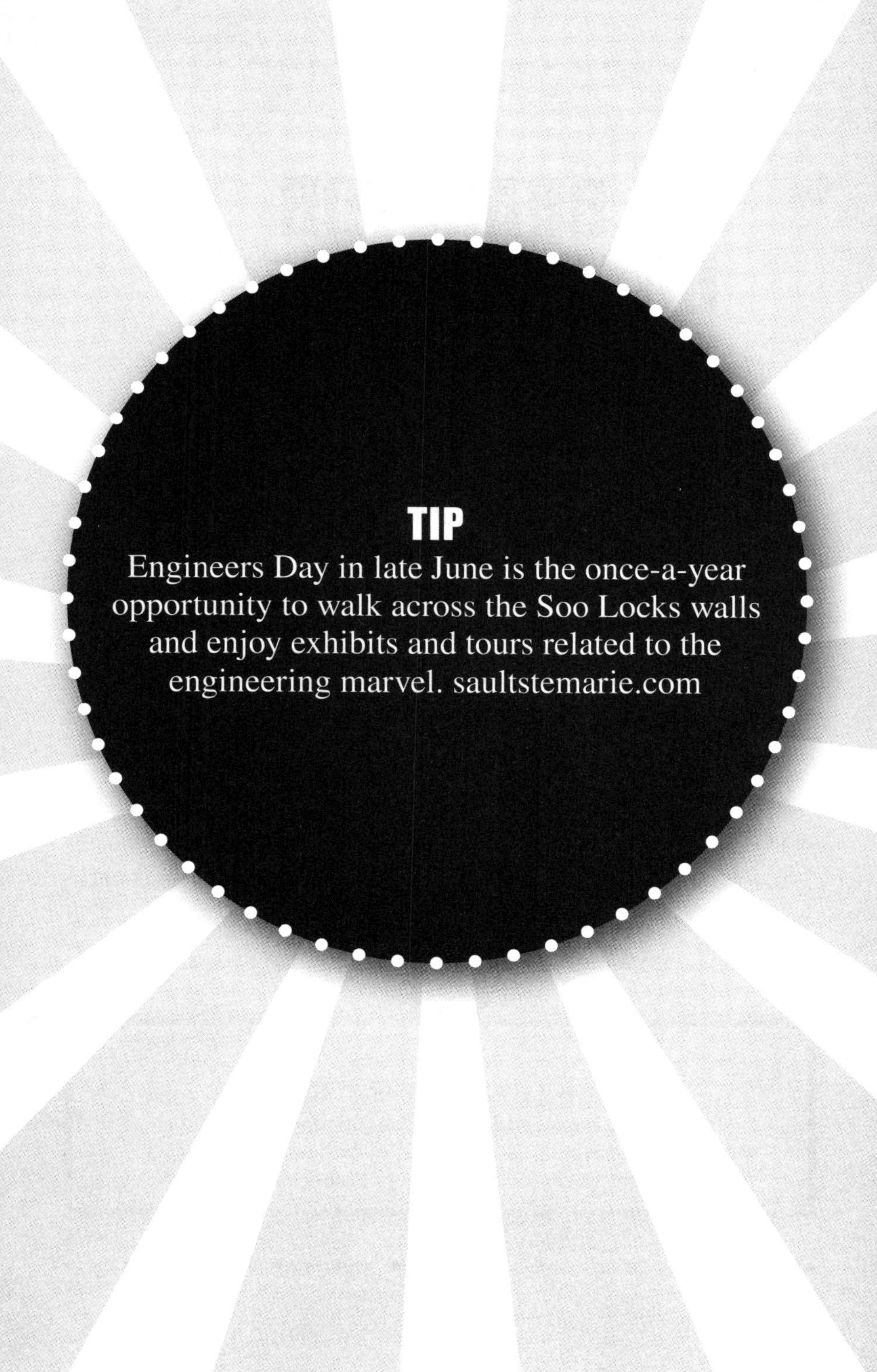
TIP
Engineers Day in late June is the once-a-year opportunity to walk across the Soo Locks walls and enjoy exhibits and tours related to the engineering marvel. saultstemarie.com

BRAKE FOR ROADSIDE SELFIES (AND GAS)

The UP is road tripper heaven. Aside from the stretch of I-75 between St. Ignace and Sault Ste. Marie, the speed limit across much of the UP's 320-mile width is mostly 55 mph. The roads are two-lane, but widened in spots for those itching to pass pokey RVs and log-hauling trucks. The slower pace makes it easier to spot and stop for tasty pasties, tourist traps, a sandy beach, the occasional hidden waterfall, or a roadside sign tempting you with Jerky-Smoked Fish-Coffee-Bait-Gas shops along the way (the UP is big, so always stop for gas). Be on the lookout for roadside, selfie-ready attractions like the towering Snow Thermometer, which measures the Keweenaw's annual white stuff (a record 390.4 inches in 1978-79), a couple of Paul Bunyans, various curio shops, and a 52-foot-tall Hiawatha—which probably was the "World's Largest Indian" when he arrived in Ironwood in 1964.

TIP

Watch for wildlife that might dart across the road, and avoid close encounters with (depending on time of day and where you're traveling) deer, moose, black bear, cougar, coyote, wolf, turkey, or any number of other critters.

MAKE TRACKS
FOR THE SNOWMOBILE MUSEUM

It's always sledding season at the Top of the Lake Snowmobile Museum in Naubinway, where volunteers have built a home for vintage and rare snow machines on loan from about 50 collectors. The 160 "old and odd" specimens on display trace the history of snow vehicles, from workhorses built to aid the fishing and forestry industries to scary-looking homemade contraptions and prototypes. A colorful assortment of recreational snowmobiles nicely represent the machines' 1960s-1970s heyday. The recent donation of 33 unique sleds by the J. Armand Bombardier Museum in Quebec required a museum expansion. The new space allows better access to a treasure trove of snowmobile sales and promotional materials, photos, vintage snow gear, and other related memorabilia.

W11660 US-2, Naubinway 49762, 906-477-6298
snowmobilemuseum.com

TIP

See sleds on display and on the move at the Antique and Vintage Snowmobile Show and Ride, held in Naubinway each February since 1993.

75

BE A LIGHTHOUSE SLEEPER

Michigan has more lighthouses—129—than any other state in the country, and some 50 of them are in the UP. Many of the photogenic sentinels are accessible for tours and to climb for sweeping views. At three of the historic beacons you can fall asleep to the sound of waves lapping—or crashing—outside your window and awaken to the solitude only a remote lighthouse can offer. The imposing 1919 Sand Hills Lighthouse—the largest light on the Great Lakes—is on the north coast of the Keweenaw Peninsula past the village of Ahmeek. Big Bay Point Lighthouse dates to 1896, and its light towers 120 feet above Lake Superior. The 1869 Portage River Lighthouse operates as the Jacobsville Lighthouse Inn and is located on a 360-foot stretch of Lake Superior shore.

LIGHTHOUSE MAPS AND INFORMATION

Search lighthouses at uptravel.com

Great Lakes Lighthouse Keepers Association

gllka.com

Big Bay Point Lighthouse Bed & Breakfast
Seven guest rooms

#3 Lighthouse Rd., Big Bay 49808, 906-345-9957
bigbaylighthouse.com

Jacobsville Lighthouse Inn
Two guest rooms

38741 Jacobs St., Lake Linden 49945, 906-523-4137
jacobsvillelighthouse.com

Sand Hills Lighthouse Inn
Eight guest rooms

6029 5 Mile Point Rd., Allouez 49901, 906-337-1744
sandhillslighthouseinn.com

PROWL
A UP GHOST TOWN

Boom-and-bust lumbering and mining industries left the UP littered with remnants of once-lively company towns like Fayette, on Lake Michigan's Garden Peninsula. Built in 1867 by the Jackson Iron Company, it was an iron smelting center until 1891. Wander its reconstructed buildings and industrial remains, preserved as a hauntingly beautiful state park. The Iron County Historical Museum's village of buildings (tavern, log cabin homestead, Victorian home, schoolhouse, and more) relocated to a former mine site isn't a ghost town, but is worth a visit. In the Western UP, restored, century-old hand-hewn log cabins offer a look at life in the Old Victoria copper mining settlement. Take a self-guided tour of several buildings of Central Mine, which, during its copper bearing years of 1854-1898, was home to 1,200 residents whose descendants return for a reunion each July.

TIP

Find information on additional Copper Country ghost towns from the Keweenaw Convention & Visitors Bureau at keweenaw.info.

Central Mine

Five miles northeast of Phoenix, off US-41, 906-289-4990
keweenawhistory.org

Fayette Historic State Park

4785 II Rd., Garden 49835, 906-644-2603
michigan.gov/fayettetownsite

Iron County Historical Museum

100 Brady Ave., Caspian 49915, 906-265-2617
ironcountyhistoricalmuseum.org

Old Victoria Historical Site

25401 Victoria Dam Rd., Rockland 49960, 906-886-2617
facebook.com/oldvictoria

MEET THE WI-FI WILDERNESS

OF MARQUETTE

It's an easy hike to the top of Sugarloaf Mountain and a perspective on the contrasts and appeal of Marquette. The UP's largest city, with a population of about 22,000, is bounded by massive Lake Superior, ancient rocks, and deep forests. It's where you can leave a crowded Wi-Fi café and, within minutes, find solitude on a mountain bike trail. Watch iron ore being loaded onto a giant freighter or see Shakespeare performed in an old boat house. Sleep in a historic downtown hotel or at a city campground. Admire century-old sandstone architecture or catch a sporting or community event at the spaceship-like, wooden Superior Dome (aka Yooperdome) on the campus of Northern Michigan University. Sip a local beer with gastro pub food of the season or grill fish fresh from the lake. Appreciate its 1840s iron mining roots and celebrate its modern magnetism.

Marquette County Convention & Visitors Bureau
117 W. Washington St., Marquette 49855, 800-544-4321 or 906-228-7749
travelmarquettemichigan.com

FIGURE OUT THE FINNISH THING

Finnish immigrants by the thousands headed to the UP to work in the mines during the copper boom, and their influence is still apparent, especially in the Keweenaw. SISU bumper stickers proclaim the Finnish traits of determination and perseverance; street signs bear multi-syllable, vowel-heavy names; and a good sweat in a sauna (rhymes with COW-na) is a revered tradition. Pannukakku, a custardy pancake, is the breakfast favorite at Suomi (Finland) Home Bakery, and the Keweenaw Co-Op carries the squeaky cheese juustoa. At Finlandia University, the Finnish American Heritage Center is a hub of cultural programming, art exhibits, and workshops open to the public. In June, juhannus bonfires mark Midsummer, and January's Heikinpäivä winter festival includes a wife-carrying contest. It's a Finn thing.

Finnish American Heritage Center
435 Quincy St., Hancock 49930, 906-487-7302
finlandia.edu/fahc

Keweenaw Co-Op
1035 Ethel Ave., Hancock 49930, 906-482-2030
keweenaw.coop

Suomi Home Bakery
54 Huron St., Houghton 49931, 906-482-3220

RUSH TO COPPER COUNTRY

Before the nation's famous Gold Rush, there was the UP's copper boom on the Keweenaw Peninsula. Large-scale mining began in 1845, and by the late 1800s "Copper Country" supplied 75 percent of the nation's copper. Immigrants came by the thousands to work in the mines: Finns, Italians, Cornish, Slovenians, Swedes, Norwegians, Irish, French-Canadians, and others—and each ethnic group had its own churches, saloons, and social activities. By 1968 the boom had gone bust. The last mine closed. The Keweenaw National Historical Park protects this legacy in association with 21 independent Keweenaw Heritage Sites related to copper history, culture, industry, or natural resources. Get oriented at the Calumet Visitor Center, where exhibits focus on the human aspect of the immigrant populations. Join a ranger-led walking tour of downtown Calumet for a good introduction for your own self-guided tour of heritage sites across the peninsula.

Keweenaw National Historical Park
Calumet Visitor Center
98 5th St., Calumet 49913, 906-483-3176
nps.gov/kewe/
Seasonal hours

GET LOST IN THE PAST
AT HANKA HOMESTEAD

Just when you think you've gone astray on a gravel road in the dense woods somewhere near the base of the Keweenaw Peninsula, a hillside clearing confirms that you are indeed lost—in the nineteenth-century world of a Finnish immigrant family. Hanka Homestead Museum, a compound of hand-hewn log structures begun in the 1890s, reveals the simple, self-reliant lives of Herman and Anna Hanka and their adult children. The Hankas farmed 40 acres and traded skills and goods, and occasionally socialized, with their few neighbors. The electricity-free house, smoke sauna, milking barn, and other outbuildings stand as they did in the 1920s. You almost expect to see Herman sipping strong coffee at the table in the spotless kitchen, the floors covered with the rag rugs and sturdy furnishings that remained when the last son, Jalmar, died in 1966.

Hanka Homestead is a Keweenaw National Historical Park site. Follow the signs from US-41 west on Arnheim Rd., about ten miles north of Baraga.

906-334-2601
hankahomesteadmuseum.org

LIVE
LIKE A COPPER KING

At a time when copper miners were making 25 cents per hour, Thomas Hoatson, owner of the Calumet & Arizona Mining Co., built a 45-room Neoclassical mansion for the sum of $50,000 in 1908. If only for a few nights, you can make yourself at home in the copper magnate's 13,000-square-foot Laurium Manor Inn, now a 10-room bed and breakfast. Lounge in the wood-beamed library; admire the stained glass, oak staircase, and tile fireplaces; and sip tea on the Corinthian-columned porch. In the morning, step into the dining room, where the walls are covered in embossed and gilded elephant hide, for a breakfast that might include almond poppy seed pancakes, cheesy herb eggs, granola, pastries, and fruit. Can't stay overnight? Stop by for a self-guided tour of the home and grounds (seasonal).

320 Tamarack St., Laurium 49913, 906-337-2549
laurium.info

TIP

Stroll around the block to see the memorial to hometown hero, Notre Dame football star George "Win one for the Gipper" Gipp. As a kid, he worked at the Michigan House Café in neighboring Calumet, where a burger bears his name.

GO UNDERGROUND
ON A MINE TOUR

There's no better way to understand the UP's copper and iron mining history than to go beneath the surface of the earth for a glimpse of a miner's dangerous, dirty, and demanding work. The Iron Mountain Iron Mine tour travels by open-air train into the "big stope," a massive cavity that produced some 22 million tons of ore between 1877 and 1945. At the Adventure Mine near Ontonagon, excursions include a family-friendly walking tour, a chance to rappel 80 feet into a mine shaft, and a strenuous five-hour exploration of remote parts of the mine. Head to the iconic Quincy Mine Shaft in Hancock for a look at the world's largest steam-powered hoist engine and take a half-mile journey into the underground copper mine. Each mine and tour is different, but all go into dark and dank environments, so plan accordingly. Tours are seasonal.

Adventure Mining Company
200 Adventure Ave., Greenland 49929, 906-883-3371
adventureminetours.com

Iron Mountain Iron Mine
W4852 US-2, Vulcan 49892, 906-563-8077
ironmountainironmine.wixsite.com/ironmine

Quincy Mine
49750 US-41, Hancock 49930, 906-482-3101
quincymine.com

TIP
Wear close-toed footwear and dress for chilly temperatures in the mines.

THE FLYiNG MOOSE™
ORGANiC FOOD, GEAR & BEER

FASHION AND SHOPPING

83

GET TRAPPED
BY DA YOOPERS

If the sign for "Free Admission – Free Bathrooms" doesn't draw you in, the massive chainsaw named Big Gus should make you brake at Da Yoopers Tourist Trap and Museum in Ishpeming. The indoor/outdoor roadside attraction is dedicated to the Yooper character as imagined by the music and comedy team whose hit tunes include "Second Week of Deer Camp" and "Rusty Chevrolet." The Tourist Trap is the ultimate source for Yooper souvenirs and novelty items—naughty and nice—as well as a selection of quality gifts, books, cribbage boards, and minerals in the Rock Knockers Rock Shop. It's not everywhere you see the likes of Big Ernie, a working rifle more than 33 feet long, which has fired a duct tape-wrapped rock two and a half miles.

490 N. Steel St. (US-41), Ishpeming 49849, 906-485-5595
dayoopers.com

84

DANGLE MOTHER NATURE
FROM YOUR EAR

The nature-inspired jewelry of Beth Millner captures the world around her, in distinctive silver, brass, gold, and copper pieces that are eco-friendly and that are made of recycled metals and salvaged copper from a former UP mine. In the studio above her downtown Marquette shop, Beth and assistants design, cast, craft, and hand-finish pendants, earrings, bracelets, and rings adorned with trees, waves, and birds. The jewelry is hand-sawn, stamped, and hammered in single pieces or layers of metal. Some designs are more elaborate, incorporating Lake Superior agates and greenstone, Michigan's state gem. Popular pendants are hammered silver or copper pieces with the outline of the UP or Lake Superior.

521 W. Washington St., Marquette 49855, 906-226-3540
bethmillner.com

BUY A FLIGHT OF FANCY
AT OPEN WINGS GALLERY

At the funky, shingled house by the side of the road in Munising, the art starts at a fence made of silvery pieces of driftwood, fills the inviting porch, and hints at the creativity of the couple behind the screened door of Open Wings Gallery. Thomas and Jill Baugnet rescued a house from ruin and transformed it into a sweet space to sell their own functional and decorative pottery, plus the works of more than 40 other UP artists. The aroma of scented soaps and candles wafts through the airy gallery, where the wood floors gleam and the walls and simple shelves are loaded with ceramics, woodcraft, birch bark items, furniture, rugs, textiles, paintings, photography, books, yard art, jewelry, clothing, and other examples of what can happen when creativity takes flight.

318 W. Munising Ave., Munising 49862, 906-387-5070
openwingspottery.com

86

BOOK IT
TO SNOWBOUND BOOKS

In a city where the average snowfall reaches 178 inches a year, the Marquette bookstore's name makes sense. You wouldn't mind if, while browsing the latest titles, staff picks, or Michigan-centric selections, a sudden blizzard hit and you were snowed in at Snowbound Books. Ray Nurmi opened the beloved indie house of books in 1984 and sold it a few years ago to Dana Schulz, a longtime employee at the hillside shop. She carries on the traditions of good and knowledgeable service, a choice inventory of "thoughtful new books, [and] quality used books," author events, book club, and community involvement that have earned the support of loyal customers.

118 N. Third St., Marquette 49855, 906-228-4448
snowboundbooks.com

TAP INTO
UP MAPLE SYRUP

It's the oldest agricultural activity in America and Michigan's first agricultural crop of the season. The maple syrup harvest runs into April in the UP, where sugar maples grow across the peninsula, and family operations bottle and sell small batches of the naturally delicious sweetener at farm markets and roadside stands. Tassier Sugar Bush in Cedarville is one of the larger producers that welcomes visitors to the family farm. Tassier also participates with other syrup producers in the annual Michigan Maple Syrup Association's Michigan Maple Weekend, a free, springtime open house and chance to tour the sugar bush, see trees tapped, and buy maple products from the source.

Tassier Sugar Bush
2875 E. Swede Rd., Cedarville 49719, 888-744-5024 or 906-484-3219
tassiersugarbush.com

Michigan Maple Weekend
michiganmapleweekend.com

88

PUT A STORMY KROMER LID ON IT

Back in 1903 in Milwaukee, railway man George "Stormy" Kromer asked his wife, Ida, to make him a hat that wouldn't fly off his head while he was working aboard the locomotives. The snug, warm cap she came up with was a hit, and a workwear fashion icon was born. From the original hat, Stormy Kromer has evolved into an expanded line of caps and sturdy, quality apparel worn by hipsters as well as Yoopers. Stormy Kromer is now based in Ironwood, where you can shop and take a tour of the factory where employees hand-stitch the original hat and its variations, all bearing the label "Made in USA in Michigan's Upper Peninsula."

1238 Wall St., Ironwood 49938, 888-455-2253
stormykromer.com

TIP

Pose for a selfie with the Paul Bunyan-sized Stormy Kromer cap located on Cloverland Drive, around the bend from the plant.

LET UP TRADING COMPANY

PUT THE YOOPER IN YOU

Express your inner Yooper at the UP Trading Company in Newberry, the official "Moose Capital of Michigan." It's stocked to the rafters with an eclectic mix of goods to support (or create) your Up North lifestyle habits, from local specialty foods to cabin décor, books, and UP-themed wearables. Stormy Kromer caps, Moose Capital T-shirts, and Yooper Girl sweatshirts share space with chic women's clothing that looks good on both sides of the Mackinac Bridge. There are home accessories and accents like birch picture frames, nature-scented candles, UP throw pillows, and folk-art birds carved locally. The adjacent Exclusive Moose carries log furniture.

223 Newberry Ave., Newberry 49868, 906-762-4042
uptradingcompany.net

BE A SHOPPER
AT COPPER WORLD

If you've been searching for a proper copper mug for your Moscow Mule, Copper World's got it. Under the roof of the 1869 John Green Block, the oldest wood frame building in Calumet, you'll find the local metal in wall art, handcrafted ornaments, kitchenware, and standout bookends. But it's not all about copper. There are locally made and nature-inspired goods like thimbleberry jam, Stormy Kromer hats, sauna soap, candles, Yooper souvenirs, and fine jewelry featuring Lake Superior agates and Isle Royale greenstone (the state gem). The selection of books, music, and DVDs related to the UP includes the coming-of-age indie movie *Superiorland*, filmed on location in the Keweenaw.

101 5th St., Calumet 49913, 906-337-4016
calumetcopper.com

FALL IN LOVE
WITH FALLING ROCK

Part coffee shop, part book haven and local art gallery, part community gathering spot, the Falling Rock Café & Bookstore in downtown Munising is hard to peg but easy to love. Housed in adjoining, renovated 1896 buildings, there are comfy places to hang out and browse the 30,000 used and new books, use the free Wi-Fi, listen to live music, and sip a Great Lakes Coffee Company drink. Menu favorites include muffins, smoked whitefish bagel, and sundaes, shakes, and ice cream by the scoop. Falling Rock is a great stop before or after a Pictured Rocks visit—the boat cruise dock is just down the block.

104 E. Munising Ave., Munising 49862, 906-387-3008
fallingrockcafe.com

ADOPT A HEAVY METAL MUSICIAN

AT ADHOCWORKSHOP

You won't know until you see him that what's missing from your life is a guitar player assembled from assorted metal parts, poised to play a rusted cast iron frypan instrument. Maybe what your yard needs is a towering, car-hood-breasted bird with an oil drum head, capped by the lid of a kettle grill. Or you could hook a fish with a beer can body and fins of scrap leather. At his adhocWORKshop in Rapid River, the wildly imaginative Ritch Branstrom puts his solid metal working skills and a heavy dose of humor to work crafting surprisingly expressive characters and creatures, big and small, from heaps of found objects. To take one of his creations home, call ahead; hours at his jam-packed gallery are by appointment, chance, or fate.

10495 S. Main St., Rapid River 49878, 906-399-1572
adhocWORKshop.com

Scott-Atw
TSJAY
GREAT LAKES 90

GET DRESSED
AT GETZ'S

Find your Sorels, plaid shirts, Stormy Kromer, and other Yooperwear under one roof at Getz's, a century-spanning clothing store in downtown Marquette. Louis Getz opened his first shop in 1879 in nearby Michigamme, but seven years later moved to the city, where his dry goods business flourished. Since 1900, Getz's Clothiers has been at home in its handsome, three-story corner building that retains the feel of an old-fashioned department store while catering to the contemporary tastes of men, women, and children with active and outdoor wear, shoes, boots, accessories, and fashion clothing. Still a family business, Getz's hallmark is its friendly, helpful service. As shopping experiences go, it's about as good as it getz.

218 S. Front St., Marquette 49855, 800-746-7438 or 906-226-3561
getzs.com

DIAL UP
SOME 906 SPIRIT

As big as the UP is, at 16,452 square miles, it has just one area code: 906. A few years ago, the 906 Hunting Company was hatched out of Tanner Flatt's love of the outdoors and an entrepreneurial dream. He was in high school. As a college student, with his family's support, he moved the growing business into a storefront in Naubinway. Inside the big log cabin, you can munch a cookie (freshly baked by Tanner's mom) while you shop 906-themed T-shirts, sweats, and hats, fishing lures, fine UP-made pocket and hunting knives, jewelry, and local art. Don't miss the pieces by woodworker Jim Rutledge, who creates wood lathe-turned bowls in basket-illusion style, which he paints with intricate designs to emulate woven Native American pieces.

W11695 US-2, Naubinway 49762, 906-477-9600
906hunt.com

95

SEEK WILDERNESS
ON IVERSON SNOWSHOES

In 1954 in the mid-peninsula village of Shingleton, Clarence Iverson began handcrafting snowshoes using local white ash, full grain rawhide, and copper hardware. Over the decades, the company changed hands a few times but continued to turn out quality snowshoes stamped with its motto, "Seek Wilderness." Iverson now produces 17 styles of wood snowshoes, open-laced with rawhide or neoprene. Its expanded product line includes nets for trout fishing and snowshoe-inspired furniture. The growing company moved up the road from its original location to Wetmore, where there's room for growth and retail sales. It just happens to be convenient to Pictured Rocks National Lakeshore, a great place to break trail on authentic UP Iverson snowshoes.

E9664 M-28, Wetmore 49895, 906-452-6370
iversonssnowshoes.com

KEEP CALM AND SHOP ON
AT THE MUSTARD SEED

As Leonard Fieber paddles his canoe into the wilderness near his UP home, he's on the lookout for sticks left by beavers after they've chewed off the bark. The gathered pieces of aspen, pine, and maple form the tables, benches, chairs, lamps, and wall art he calls Beaver Chew Furniture. You can find his contemporary rustic furnishings at The Mustard Seed Gift Store & Art Loft in Manistique, a place of "hospitality, peace, and beauty" created more than 25 years ago by co-owners Cathy Jerde and Cindy King. A wide, open staircase leads to the loft gallery of paintings, photography, and pottery by local artists, while the main floor is filled with a pleasant assortment of home goods, soy candles, books, jewelry, Great Lakes wearables, and too-pretty-to-use soaps.

237 S. Cedar St., Manistique 49854, 906-341-5826
facebook.com/themustardseed.manistique

STOCK UP ON GOOD STUFF

AT A MODERN GENERAL STORE

The Flying Moose in downtown Marquette is a one-stop lifestyle shop that caters to a love of good, clean eating and enjoying the great outdoors. To-go sandwiches, soups, salads, and bakery treats adhere to the "healthy and wholesome" philosophy that extends to the bins, crates, jars, and shelves stocked with condiments, snacks, chocolate, bulk spices, tea, and coffee. Produce, meat, poultry, eggs, and maple syrup are mostly organic and sourced from area farmers and producers. The beer assortment is heavy on Michigan craft brews, and the wines are reasonably priced. The Flying Moose rents and retails bikes, and sells hiking and camping gear, kayaks, longboards, backpacks, compasses, hammocks, goods crafted by local artists, and a bunch of other cool stuff you'd expect to find at a modern general store.

351 W. Washington St., Marquette 49855, 906-273-2246
theflyingmooseup.com

EXPRESS YOUR UFF DA
IN NORWAY

If you're looking for Scandinavian imports, head to Norway. The old iron mining town near the Wisconsin border is probably best known for nearby whitewater rafting and hiking along the dramatic Piers Gorge and Menominee River. But in a handsome grey house on a hill, the Swedish Passport Company/Scandia House International is filled with quality imports, from Norwegian Uff da wares to painted Swedish Dala horses, collectible Danish Christmas plates, intricately patterned Icelandic sweaters, and Iittala glass from Finland. It requires circling the rooms a few times to take in the dizzying array of goods; every corner is filled with cookbooks, kitchen and glassware, Baltic amber jewelry, clogs, textiles, imported foods, candies, knitwear, and sauna supplies—all tidily arranged, of course.

626 Iron St., Norway 49870, 906-563-8200
swpassport.com

LET YOUR SWEET TOOTH GO BONKERS FOR DONCKERS

Gold lettering splashed across the retro green-and-black storefront announces "Candies-Lunches-Sodas." A red neon sign boasts "Finer Candies." Step over the threshold where Donckers is spelled out in mosaic tiles, and step into a delicious taste of Marquette's past. Fred Donckers started selling his handmade candies from a cart in 1896, and in 1914 he opened the confectionery that still bears his name. The deep, narrow sweet shop has been authentically restored, with high tin ceilings and original wood floors. Vintage glass-shelved cases display truffles, toffees, barks, and signature sea salt caramels. Come for the candy, and stay for a phosphate, sundae, or malt at the old-fashioned soda fountain. Donckers also serves breakfast and sandwiches—ask for the three-meat club that President Obama enjoyed during his visit in 2011.

137 W. Washington St., Marquette 49855, 906-226-6110
donckersonline.com

TIP

If you enjoy custom-made sweets, the candy makers at Sayklly's, an Escanaba-based confectioner since 1906, make chocolate Yooper Bars that are sold at its shops and across the UP.

1304 Ludington St., Escanaba 49829, 906-786-1524
saykllys.com

100

HANG THE NORTHERN LIGHTS
ON YOUR WALL

Shawn Malone's spectacular images of the northern lights have a loyal following online and at her Lake Superior Photo gallery in downtown Marquette. She gained worldwide attention when her time-lapse video "North Country Dreamland" was the People's Choice winner in a Smithsonian online competition. For the seven-minute video, set to soothing music, she selected and edited 10,000 still images of the UP sky. Yes, Shawn takes a lot of photos. Besides showcasing the aurora borealis and the night sky, she points her camera at natural and scenic wonders throughout the seasons, focusing mainly on the Lake Superior region. Stop at her gallery for a mounted, ready-to-hang art print, and put the northern lights under your roof.

211 S. Front St., Marquette 49855, 906-228-3686
facebook.com/lakesuperiorphoto

SUGGESTED
ITINERARIES

DIG INTO MINING HERITAGE

SOFT ADVENTURING

UP FOR EXTREME ADVENTURE

FUN WITH THE FAMILY

FOR THE TWO OF YOU

GET BACK TO NATURE

YOOPER CULTURE, EH?

UNIQUE TO THE UP

ACTIVITIES
BY SEASON

SPRING

SUMMER

FALL

WINTER

INDEX